FINDING IT

WANDA TORRES

© 2019 Wanda Torres

Printed in the United States of America

ISBN: 978-1-7339405-7-3

All rights reserved as sole property of the author. The author guarantees all content is original and does not infringe upon the legal rights of any other person or work. No part of this book may be reproduced, stored in a retrieval system, or transmitted in any form or by any means, without expressed written permission of the author.

Published by: The Ghost Publishing

Author: Wanda Torres

1

Apparently, I was a troubled child. My bad behavior first showed up when I was a freshman... well, that was what everyone said. During my first year at Starborough High School, in Camden, Maine, I was ordered to in-school suspension *twenty-two times* and suspended, *twice*. Not exactly an accomplishment to brag about—they don't hand out trophies for that kind of record-breaking.

I think that was what pushed my mother to the edge... the suspensions. One after another. To her, it was like I'd gone down the path for unruly kids. Her attitude was that I'd skipped right past misdemeanors and went straight to committing felonies. She had gotten so upset, she even told me the only thing I would do right was to get arrested.

Truth be told, I didn't have a good reason for what happened that year.

I'd been picked on a lot in junior high school. I don't know why it happened. Nothing stood out about me... I wasn't fat, I didn't wear glasses, or have braces—the weaknesses that bullies usually preferred in their victims.

I played field hockey and lacrosse, as a starter on both teams.

But, even with my teammates, I didn't fit in... never had any real friends. My two brothers would be there, but that's a family obligation.

Going into high school, I was determined to make sure I didn't suffer anymore tormenting. Whether classmates respected me, feared me, or just thought I was crazy, it didn't matter. If they'd just leave me alone, *mission accomplished*.

After I was suspended—on the last day of school, for fighting—my father, Lucas Sentmore, took an offer to transfer and opened a new office for the realty company.

Going into my sophomore year, I sat on the floor of my new bedroom surrounded by boxes and a few pieces of furniture. Just wondering what was next; I could not repeat the previous year.

"Hey, you."

I looked up to the open door. My brother leaned against the doorframe, a typical posture of his.

"Hey, Leland, you done unpacking already?"

"No. I still have a bunch to do. Just takin' a break. How are you feeling?"

Surprisingly, I think he was the only one who ever asked me that. But I couldn't think of a solid answer, so I shrugged. Leland sat down in front of me.

He could read me pretty well, so I was sure he saw the stress on my face,

"Should I bribe Dad's boss for another transfer?"

That was so Leland, making a joke of a serious moment. After a chuckle, I shook my head.

"Leona, this move is a big adjustment for all of us. You can get through this. Just keep your grades up and play sports. In time, you'll find out why you feel so... separated."

"What, like *divine destiny*?" I asked, mockingly.

Leland shrugged. "I don't know... maybe." He grinned.

"Yeah, right. Hey, do you think—"

Mom breezed in, interrupting me. "Isn't it *so* wonderful out here? Just look at that view." She swept across my room to stand by my bedroom window, looking at the trees. The leaves had started changing with the crisp autumn weather. I followed her gaze to the riotous blotches of green, yellow, orange, and red foliage. "I can write a whole new series of books just *looking* at this scenery."

My mom, Lillian Sentmore, as an author, saw things as an artist does. "This environment will help me write a new best seller." Woodstock, Vermont seemed to be good for her.

"Best seller for sure," Dad said, walking in.

Leland knew what was coming. He nudged me on the shoulder and left the room.

Dad started in first. "Listen, honey. School starts next week. To be honest, I'm worried about you. Are you going to be okay?"

I didn't want to talk about it. Like, any teen ever did. "I'm fine. It's just..." I let the words trail off, not wanting to be lectured, *again*. I sighed, rolled my eyes, and said, "It won't happen again. *Promise*."

Mom, looking unconvinced, added, "I should hope not, young lady. We raised you better than that. Your actions last year were completely unnecessary."

"I *said* it wasn't going to happen again. The fact that we are still talking about it is what's unnecessary." That sort of slipped out.

"That is exactly the kind of attitude that we are talking about. If we get any negative feedback from the school, we are going to pull you off the sports teams."

I nodded mutely, hoping I showed the right amount of meekness to convince her. Hoping I could keep my promise.

"Well then, your father and I are going out tonight."

"Would you like to join us?" Dad asked.

"No... thank you, Dad. I'm going to finish unpacking."

Left alone with my thoughts, I considered Mom's threat. I understand that with actions came consequences. But taking away field hockey and lacrosse would just be cruel. The only thing I was good at was sports.

As a freshman, I'd started on the JV team for field hockey. I would have been a starter for lacrosse, too, but, by spring, those suspensions had disqualified me from playing anything. My father had been my coach for both sports in junior high. He used to say that I had *raw talent*. In the beginning, people said that I had been made a starter because my father was the coach. Later, I happily proved them wrong when I made forty-seven percent of the season's points.

Still, nothing ever really felt right. Almost like something was missing from my life. When Dad was my coach, we'd found a common ground, but that was about the only time. I did connect with my brothers Logan and Leland. I could always talk to them.

Logan was the "I'll give you advice—take it or leave it" type. I think that was why he ended up becoming a history teacher in Starborough. Leland was more the "in your face" type. Once, in the sixth grade, a boy walked by and pushed me into the lockers. He kept walking, only to be faced with Leland. They ended up fighting. After that, boys changed from physically bullying me to verbal assaults. I guess that was better.

At 10:00pm, I figured I was done unpacking for the night. I decided to give Logan a call.

"Hey, little lady," he said.

"Hey Logan, what are you doing?"

"Nothing much. Just some school stuff. Are you settled in yet?"

"Almost. Can I ask you something?"

"Shoot."

"Why didn't you move here with us? You're so far now." Two-hundred and sixty miles to be exact.

"I don't know. Why did you act up last year?"

"Logaaan..." I whined, drawing out the word.

"I've already established my life out here." He spoke firmly. "But you've got no choice but to be there, you might as well as make the best of it." Well, that sounded more like an all-grown-up Mr. Sentmore than my brother Logan.

"You don't have a *life* out there, you only have a *job* out there.

Finding It

You can always get another one here. Who's going to tame Mom for me? You know you're her favorite."

He laughed. "I'm her favorite because I'm out on my own and didn't give her hell my entire childhood." I heard a TV playing in the background. "Look, I'll be there for the holidays. We'll go out when I visit. Have you checked out the area yet?"

I resented the whole childhood jab, but let it go. "No, Mom and Dad are out roaming around now. I'm sure Lee and I will go out before the week is up. Field hockey tryouts are the Tuesday after school starts. I can't wait."

"I'm sure you'll be a starter again this year."

"Yeah, I'll let you go. I'm exhausted and the bed is calling my name."

"Okay, little one. Be good, be safe, behave and be great at what you do."

"Thanks. Good night."

FOUR DAYS since we'd moved to Woodstock, Leland and I were in the car on our way to "get lost" in town, as Lee put it. He figured a Friday night was the best night to bump into people our age. I guessed it would do some good to meet a few people. I thought maybe I'd fit in better here.

"So, you ready for the season?" Leland's voice snapped me back to reality.

"Definitely," I answered. "I checked Moywood's field hockey record for last season. They finished twelve and six. I just might get a few field hockey scholarships, after all. Are you going out for football this season?"

"I think so. They don't have a great team, but I'm pretty sure they already have their first-string tight ends."

"But you're a *Sentmore*. A team isn't a team without a Sentmore,"

I said, mimicking our father. We laughed. "So, what are we having for dinner?"

"I looked online. I found a pizza diner in town. Supposed to be a hang-out spot. It's on a strip. So, I figure we park and walk there. Stop at a few stores on the way."

"Sounds good." After a moment of silence, I asked, "Has Mom and Dad been bothering you about college?"

"Of course they have. They started in with that last year."

I wait, expecting more. Finally, I nudged his shoulder. "Well?"

He shrugged.

"Lee, you *graduate* this year."

"I have thought about it. College was for Logan... not for me." He looked at me and sighed at the puzzled look on my face. "If I tell you what I'm going to do... you promise not to tell Mom and Dad?"

I nodded and crossed my heart. "I'm thinking... I'm going to join the military."

My mouth dropped open. "Mom is going to freak."

He glanced out the side window. "I'm almost certain that's what I'm going to do. I just haven't decided which branch."

I didn't know what to say. It was a great move. It was a solid move. It would certainly be nice to have a hero brother, but I only had Logan and Leland. If he joined the military, I would be left alone. I'd be lucky to see either of them, even once a year.

Leland parked the car and turned to face me, waiting for a response.

"Nothing would make me prouder than to have a soldier brother. But I'm not too thrilled at the idea of seeing you even less than I see Logan. When Logan went to USM, at least I got to see him every month."

He opened his door, and we both got out of the car. He walked around the front to join me on the sidewalk, obviously giving him time to think. "So... you're more worried at how often you'll get to see me than if I'll be sent overseas?"

I blew out my breath. "You get straight As. You'll probably end up behind a computer somewhere," I said, somewhat ashamed of my own neediness.

Leland pushed me, then pulled me close into a hug. "If I didn't know any better, I would say you're worse than Mom." He laughed, then, a moment later, sighed. "You'll find a few friends and you'll forget all about me, promise."

I had my doubts, but I didn't care to continue the conversation. I looked down the road for diversion. The streetlights were old-fashioned-looking lamps. The road was designed with two trees between each lamp. The brick buildings were all two-story and, on street level, had large windows for people to window-shop. We passed clothing stores, convenience stores, a candy store, and an ice cream parlor. We even saw a few restaurant and cafes. We spotted the pizza diner across the street, but Lee insisted we tour the entire strip before stopping to eat.

At the end of the business section, we started to cross the street. I heard music. Music that wasn't like anything I'd heard before. I found myself standing between two propped-open doors. Looking into a lobby I saw closed, millwork-wooden double-doors with windows. I couldn't make out what was beyond the doors, but it sounded like a concert.

I heard Leland say, "Agape Pentecostal Church of God."

I followed his gaze. He'd read what was painted on the huge window.

"Hey, service just started, do you want to join them?" he asked sarcastically. He turned away, heading back toward the pizza place. I gave one more glance into the church then followed Leland.

We got to the diner and it was packed. Even with the large amount of people, we managed to find a table. After a waiter took our order, we looked around to take it all in. Apart from some of the employees, no one was over the age of twenty-five.

Groups of people sat, bunched around tables like in a high school cafeteria. A few of the tables held so many people, they sat crowded shoulder-to-shoulder. I knew the group behind my brother must be on a sports team. They were wearing lettermen jackets and talking about the upcoming season.

The waitress arrived with our milkshakes. She assured us that she would deliver the pizza as soon as it was out. I continued to look around. The décor had a retro-fifties feel and look to it. The floor was tiled in white and black checkerboard. The walls were painted a light peach color. Red and white vinyl covered the booth seats and chairs. I noticed a jukebox a few feet from the cash registers. After taking it all in, I turned back to look at Leland, who was talking to one of the guys who wore a lettermen jacket. I tuned into their conversation while Lee was talking.

"Yeah, I played back in Maine. We just moved to town Monday." Of course, they would be talking about football.

"And who is this pretty lady?" The guy asked, looking my way.

"That's my sister, Leona. She's a sophomore this year."

"Name's Rodney." He stood, leaned over and extended his hand to shake mine.

When he stood, I noticed how tall he was. And, with plenty of muscles, I got the idea that he lifted weights. His short brown, curly hair went beautifully with his light caramel skin. Light brown eyes and beautiful white smile rounded out his good looks.

I stretched my hand to meet his. "Nice to meet you, Rodney. You play football as well?"

"Yeah, I'm co-captain of the team. Brad over there..." He pointed to a dirty-blonde-haired guy who wore a girl under each arm. "He's the quarterback and captain. I play wide receiver. You playing anything this fall?"

"Field hockey. I normally play center mid-fielder, but I'll play wherever they put me."

"Moywood only has one field hockey team. The school is too small to have both a varsity and JV team. Sorry to say, not a lot of sophomores make the cut."

"I will," I said without any hesitation. Rodney stared; his eyebrows furrowed. I could tell he was taken aback by my determined response. "I'm not cocky. Just confident." Just then, the pizza just showed up. I was glad to see it, for more than one reason.

"Well, I hope you make it," he said.

I nodded and grabbed a slice of pizza. Rodney turned to Leland. "I'm sure I'll see you around on Monday. Tryouts start Tuesday, after school. I'll message you my e-mail and you can send me your video clips. I'll forward them to coach. Hopefully, we can put in a few good words about you before tryouts."

"Sounds good." Lee shook Rodney's hand and turned to eat. Rodney returned to his group. We ate, then played few arcade games. Lee and I met a few more people. We just kind of hung out. It was just past nine-forty-five and a new wave of people had just walked in. I was ready to go. I looked to where Lee was and, like a chameleon, he'd blended in so quickly, talking with the group we figured out was last year's first-string football team.

I started walking toward my brother and, halfway there, I bumped into someone. Whoever it was, she dropped a bunch of pamphlets on the floor.

"Oh, I'm so sorry. Here, let me help you." I bent down to help pick up the papers.

"No worries. Just an accident."

We finish collecting the pamphlets. I stood up and handed her what I'd collected. Seeing her face, I noticed that something about her was different. It's like she glowed. A girl on the shorter side, with short, straight black hair, she looked almost Asian, but with caramel skin.

"Hey. You're new around here, aren't you?"

I nodded bashfully.

"My name is Eve." She held her hand out to me.

I shook her hand. "Leona."

"That's a beautiful name. Will you be joining us at Moywood high this year?"

"Yes. I'm a sophomore."

"Oh, me too!" She acted so happy about it. Almost over-the-top happy. "Maybe we'll have a few classes together." Eve grinned.

"I don't know my schedule yet. Apparently, I'll get it Monday." Leland called to me from the door. "Oh, that's my brother. I have to go. Sorry, again." I pointed at the stack in her hands.

"Here, take one and we'll call it even." She handed me a pamphlet.

I put it into my pocket, said *thank you*, and weaved my way to the door.

On the way home, we discussed the people we'd met. Lee had already made plans for the next night. He was going to meet up with some of the football players at a pool hall. He asked me to go with him to be his partner. But I declined. I figure it's best to stay under the radar until tryouts. He asked me who Eve was, but all I knew was her name and that she was in the same grade.

We got home. After giving my mother a brief summery of our outing, I went to my room. I emptied my pockets into my desk drawer, ready to take a shower.

Something about that Eve girl was different. I couldn't shake trying to figure her out. Maybe she was genuinely happy. That was pretty rare, in my experience. I guess I would have to get to know her to really figure it out. Even then, I didn't know if I wanted to do that. We'd moved to a completely different state and I haven't managed to fit in yet. Maybe that was just the way I was made. For now, all I knew was that I was tired.

Sports were the only sure thing I had to look forward to. I crawled into bed, remembering the first time we'd all gone snowboarding. I was in the sixth grade. We took the trip for Logan's senior year, as a family Christmas gift. Logan had been doing well in school and had been allowed to bring a friend on the trip. Lee and I took classes to learn how to snowboard while my parents, Logan and his friend all took off.

The instructor took us to a small hill for the class. After the basic instructions, it was time to test our skills. I fell, face first, about a third of the way down the hill. I got up and tried again. When the same thing kept happening, I asked the instructor what I was doing wrong. He told me and I tried again. By the end of our two-hour class, I had gone down the small slope over a dozen times without falling.

We had three more days on that trip and I was determined to go down the expert slope at least once. The next day, I stood at the beginner's slope. The next day, I moved up to the intermediate slope. This was where I ended up staying. Logan caught me trying to get to the expert slope. The whole day, he and his friend kept me from going any further. I fell a bunch of times, nothing serious. But I got a handle on it by our last day. From then on, it was smooth riding every time we went to the mountains.

I wished I was more active. I wished I had something physical to occupy me year-round. I'd figure that out later. For now, it was off to the clouds to dream.

Just as I was about to nod off, an image of Eve popped into my brain. She still had that *glow* and still smiled. I'd figure out her mystery.

2

The rest of the weekend was uneventful. I did go to the office with my father on Sunday. He asked me what my plans where for after high school. It wasn't until yesterday that I realized that I'd never really thought about it. I'd always managed to keep my grades in the B and C range. I'd brought home a few Ds last year. The only As I'd managed to pull were from art, gym, and music. The only thing I was good at was sports, but I didn't think that was logically a good career move. No way was I a *people* person. Here I sat, in the school's main office, full of people and I shouldn't feel anymore alone. *Shouldn't your career be something you enjoy?*

"Leona Sentmore?"

"That's me." I stood.

"My name is Mr. Cavalier. I'm the principal." We shook hands. "Let's go to my office."

We walked a short distance. In his office, there was a woman already sitting in front of the desk.

"Have a seat, please." Mr. Cavalier closed the door behind us. As I sat, he said, "This is Ms. Lumina, your guidance counselor."

"I'm sorry. Did you say my *guidance counselor*?"

"Yes, I did."

Finding It

I glanced at her and she smiled.

"After looking at your transcripts and talking with your parents, we felt it best for you to have someone to talk to," Mr. Cavalier said.

"No disrespect... but you thought a guidance counselor was the best option?" I was amazed at how logical they assumed they were being. I turned to Ms. Lumina and said, "Talking to you, a stranger that..." I paused and sighed. I could tell by their expressions that I wasn't being offered a choice. "I'm just not comfortable with this."

"Well, Leona. May I call you by your first name?" Ms. Lumina asked.

I nodded, only because I was done talking.

"We will meet every other week during your study hall period on Wednesdays. If you can demonstrate, by the holidays, that there is no reason to continue, then we won't." She was unusually soft-spoken.

She made me feel slightly suspicious. But I pressed my lips together and nodded again.

"Good." Mr. Cavalier shuffled some papers and selected one. "Here is your schedule. Ms. Lumina will take you to your first class. After that, an honor student by the name of *Thomas* will be showing you to the rest of the classrooms. Any questions?"

"Yes. I don't see any gym class on my schedule."

"It's my understanding that you play sports."

I nodded.

"In this school, if you play on one of the teams, you're exempted from gym. If by chance you don't end up on a team, talk to Ms. Lumina and she'll get your schedule changed. Here at Moywood, if you get anything less than a C average, you're pulled off the team."

"What?" I jerked forward, shocked at the thought of losing sports.

"It's a rule that applies to everyone in this school. From what your parents tell me, sports is a passion of yours. We see it as a vantage point... you can look at it as motivation."

My parents talk too much.

"Okay, well, enjoy your first day."

Both Ms. Lumina and I walked through the halls to my first class. I walked, looking down at my schedule. Every day was the same, except third period. I had Spanish II, English II, then third period alternated through the week between art, music, and study hall. After I lunch, it was algebra, world history, and then biology. It looked easy enough. I only had to remember the third period changes.

"Does your schedule look all right?"

I knew she was just trying to be nice. I doubt she liked her job enough to actually care. In the past, every time I'd opened up to someone, it always came back to haunt me. I was not going to fall into this trap. "It's fine."

"I know this isn't your ideal situation, but you can trust me, Leona."

"*Really?*" I said it with enough attitude that she has to know I didn't believe her. "How many of your students have you used that line with?"

"Every single one of them."

Surprised, I blinked. I didn't know what I expected her to say, but it sure wasn't that. I thought she was telling the truth. We'd arrived at a closed classroom door. I looked at Ms. Lumina, square in the eye, looking for a lack of sincerity, but didn't find any.

"I say that to my students because it's *true*. I guess, in time, you'll figure it out on your own." She smiled and held open the door for me.

After a brief introduction, Ms. Lumina left and I took a seat. The Spanish teacher, Mr. Sanchez, handed out textbooks. He covered his expectations and rules, then assigned us lockers. Just then, a student walked in. Standing with his back to me, I noticed his jet black, spiked-up hair and caramel skin. I thought nothing of it and went back to filling in some paperwork. Just then the bell rang. As I made my way to the door, Mr. Sanchez called my name.

When I got to his desk, Mr. Sanchez said, "This is Maka. He'll be showing you the way to your next class."

Something about the guy seemed vaguely familiar. "I was told that someone named *Thomas* was going to show me around."

"That's me. My first name is Thomas. But, everyone calls me Maka."

"That's quite a difference from Thomas." I'd meant to say that to myself.

He smiled. "My middle name is Makaio. I guess people got lazy about saying the whole name. So, Maka it is."

"Oh, okay. Ummm, I kind of wanted to take a crack at locating my locker. Do we have time for that?"

"Sure. What's the locker number?"

"Two-eighty-eight."

"Okay, follow me."

Tall and well built, he definitely played football.

"So where are you from?" he asked.

"Maine."

"Do you miss it?"

"Not really. No."

Maka laughed. "That bad, huh?"

I shrugged.

He stopped. "Here's your locker."

I opened the locker and began putting my stuff in it. It didn't seem like he was from around here, either. "Were you born here?"

"No, I was born in Hawaii. We moved here when I was in the seventh grade."

"I don't even have to ask. I know you miss it."

"I sure do. Especially around wintertime." He got a wistful look on his face. "We go back every year for either winter or spring break. What's your next class?"

I closed the locker and snapped the lock shut. My eyes dropped to my schedule. "English with Mr. Warren."

"He's new this year. Does it say what room he's in?"

"Two-zero-two."

"Oh." He turned around and pointed to a door. "That's it."

We walked a few feet, but just short of the entrance, I stopped. "I think I can handle it from here."

"I'll wait out here for you after class then?"

I nodded, went in a took a seat.

Eve came in and sat next to me. "How are you?"

"I'm good." She still seemed happy. "So, my brother is showing you to your classes? Is he being nice?"

"Huh?"

"My brother Maka. He's showing you around, right?"

I knew he looked familiar. Those two could be twins. "Yes. He's fine."

Just then, the teacher called for the class's attention. He handed out a list of books we'd be reading this year. The second piece of paper was vocabulary and the assignment for those words. The instructions were, "Create the shortest story you can—using all of the vocabulary words." The book we'd be reading was *The Great Gatsby*.

"Thank God these titles are so much better. Last year we read *The Odyssey, Once in a Future King,* and *Macbeth*." Eve sighed and shook her head. "The only two I enjoyed were *The Giver* and *The Hatchet*."

I whispered, "It doesn't look too bad. I've already read three of these."

Eve smiled. "Apparently you enjoy reading."

"Do you ladies have any questions?" Mr. Warren's voice broke through into our conversation. I looked up and noticed everyone was staring.

"No, sir. I was just looking over the list of books and I realized that I've already read three of them."

He looks at me pensively. "Really, which ones?"

"*Of Mice and Men, Speak,* and *Tuesday with Morrie*."

"Interesting. Well I guess you don't have much choice for the winter vacation. Come January, I'll have another book picked out for you."

There goes my *easy A* for January. "Yes, sir."

I anxiously waited for the bell. When it rang, Eve and I got up. As promised, Maka was waiting just outside the door.

"Hey Maka," she said with a playful tone. "Whatcha up to?"

"Nothing. You get anything interesting?" Eve shook her head. Then he turned to me. "What's your next class?"

"Art with Mr. Littmen."

Both Eve and Maka said, "Oooooo... his class is fun."

Eve continued. "I spent *all year* last year trying to get that perfect grade." Just then, the bell rang for the five-minute warning. She rushed off. "Enjoy the class. Lord knows, I'm dreading calculus."

Maka walked beside me. "What was Eve talking about? The *perfect grade*?"

"Mr. Littmen offers a perfect A-grade for anyone who can surprise him with their art. He's kind of old and been teaching for a long time. He swears he's seen it all."

My mind was already busy thinking of a surprise project.

Maka broke in. "Don't think too hard just yet. You need your place of origin. When you get to class, you'll have to take a piece of paper from a box. On the paper there will be a place or country written on it. All your work has to be inspired by that place."

"Do you have him this year?"

He shook his head. "I have Ms. Gates this year. I had him freshmen year."

"What were your places?"

"First half of the year, I had Germany. Second, I had the Czech Republic."

"Czech Republic sounds hard."

"After doing a few building and landscape pieces, Mr. Littmen told me I had to start getting creative or my A would deteriorate —fast."

"Maybe that's the whole point. To get you to think outside of typical drawing and sculpting subjects."

He shrugged. "Maybe... this is it. You have lunch next period?"

I nodded.

"I'll wait out here, then."

"Okay." I turned and saw Mr. Littman holding a box. He said to grab a paper but not to open it yet. I did and found a seat up front. I needed to get every detail of this challenge. I didn't know how yet, but I was going to win this *perfect grade*. The bell rang and people shuffled to their seats.

Mr. Littman set down the box. "Hello, students. I trust you have all enjoyed your summer vacation."

Mumbled replies echoed around the room.

"Most of you already know how my class works but..." He glanced at me. "For those of you who are new and for those who have amnesia, each of your papers have a place written on it. That is your place of origin. That is where you will take inspiration from... until the end January. I expect three art pieces to be turned into me every week. Now for the challenge. I'm old and have seen it all."

At least one guy snorted. A few higher-pitched giggles sounded muffled, like girls trying to stifle it with their hand.

Mr. Littman ignored them. "So, the student who surprises me with their artwork will get a perfect grade for the whole year. No limits to how many times you try. Should someone win, you are still required to come to class. Even though it won't be graded, you still have to turn in assignments."

Half of the students booed.

"There are supplies throughout the classroom, use whatever you choose. I am here for anyone needing help. After you have looked at your place of origin, please return your paper to the box, let me know what it is then begin on your first piece. You may now look at your papers."

With uncontrolled anticipation, I look at my paper. Ironically, I got Hawaii. *Okay... Hawaii. Volcanos, flowers, hula dancers, beaches, surfing, sugar cane, macadamias.* Whatever I entered for this challenge—it can't be any of those things. If I thought of it that fast then so did a million other kids. I took the paper back to Mr. Littmen's desk and set it in the box. "Mr. Littman, the pieces we hand in for the challenge... does it still have to be inspired by the place of origin?"

"Yes, it does. What did you get?"

"Hawaii." He wrote it down next to my name on the attendance sheet.

"Only one student can win the perfect grade, correct?"

"Only one."

"Are there any rules to what we hand in for the challenge?"

"Just that your inspiration has to be of Hawaii."

"Anything goes?"

"Anything goes." Mr. Littman looked over his glasses and smiled.

Back at my seat, I began a list of ideas. But even then, everything I wrote seemed mediocre. If I wanted to win this, I had to get to know Hawaii. Get to know the culture and history of it. I wasn't good at drawing. Sculpting remained my strong suit. The bell rang but I lingered. "Mr. Littman, I have a few more questions if you don't mind."

"Not at all."

"If I hand in something for the challenge, does it also count for my grade?"

"No. Your assignments and the challenge are two different things. If you hand something in for the challenge you need to specify that it's for the challenge. Otherwise I'll grade it."

"What if I wanted to sculpt something? Obviously, sculpting takes a long time. Is it possible to have what I sculpt count for the week?"

"I'm fairly firm about three pieces every week. Most people can draw a few things while working on a sculpture."

"Sure, if you want my grade to go from an A to an F."

He chuckled. "If you think that what you are working on should suffice for the week, come and talk to me. Although I am inclined to say if you don't practice drawing, you'll never get good at it."

"I'll practice. Just not at the expense of my grade." I noticed Maka walking in. "Okay, well at some point I would like to make a chess board. I'll sculpt the pieces. Would you allow that to count for the week?"

Maka stopped next to me. I noticed that Mr. Littman seemed to be surprised by something. "You look surprised, Mr. Littman. Does that mean I get the perfect grade?"

He laughed a loud, hearty laugh. "I'll tell you what. If you make a chess board, I will allow it to count for the week."

"Great. Okay. So, umm, I'll see you Friday."

Just as Maka and I walked into the hallway, Eve showed up. "So where did you get?"

"Ironically," I answered, "Hawaii."

"Go figure," Maka said.

Eve jumped in. "Well hey, if you need help, my family is your best resource. Do you have lunch now?" I nodded. "Great. We can eat together."

In the lunchroom, we grabbed our meals and sat with Maka and a few of his friends. The boys started talking about a tournament. Curious, I turned to Eve. "What are they talking about? A tournament?"

"Maka and his friends compete in different martial arts. Next month they are going to a jiu jitsu tournament."

"Do you compete?"

She smiled. "I compete in kickboxing and Maui Thai only. I tried out for field hockey last year and didn't make the team. So, I started training at the gym." She shrugged.

"Do you plan on trying out tomorrow?"

"Sure. I went to field hockey camp over the summer. Hopefully, it helped enough to get me onto the team."

"If you make it, maybe Friday we can get together for some one-on-one."

"Can't Friday. I have church. But I am free Saturday. You can join me for church Friday and I'll join you for field hockey Saturday. Assuming we both make the team." I was amazed at how upbeat this girl could be. Even when talking about something that may not even happen.

"Count me out Friday. I'm in for Saturday, though."

"Why not Friday?"

"I don't know... the whole *God thing*," I wiggled my eyebrows. "Seems a little farfetched to me. One person knowing everything about everything. I just don't buy it. So, I don't give it much thought."

Still upbeat, she pursed her lips. "Can I ask you a few questions?"

"Sure."

"When you look at a building you know that its creator is an architect, right?" I nodded. "That architect knows everything about that building. Its dimensions, the material it's made of, and so on. Right?" I nodded again. "For something to have a beginning there has to be an independent source to help create it. In this case, the building has its beginning and the architect is the independent source." She raised her eyebrows looking to see if I followed her logic.

"Right," I said.

"Both science and the Bible agree that the universe had a beginning. Now for that to hold true, the universe needs an independent source. Is it really that farfetched for its architect? For the independent source to be God?"

"Yeah, but for one person to know *everything*." I shook my head. *Not buying it,* I thought.

"For a person to know everything about everything. You're right, that is farfetched. But that's the beauty of God. He isn't a *person*. If

He was, He wouldn't be so dependable. He's just the one and only true God."

I always had something to say... so what was wrong with me now? I opened my mouth to say... I didn't even know what. Just then, the bell rang. Literally saved by the bell.

Maka and I walked to my algebra class. Eve went the opposite way. The rest of the day passed without any issues. Eve and I have world history and biology together. She didn't mention the God thing again. She stayed upbeat and smiley the whole time. It was refreshing. Seemed like most people were always angry or gloomy about something. Maybe her optimism would rub off.

After school, I sat on the car waiting for Leland. With the rush of cars and students, it was hard to locate him. He eventually showed up. Mom was waiting for us at home. You would think that, after three kids, she'd be more relaxed—but she wasn't. We humored her a bit. Told her about our day. We ate dinner without Dad—he was stuck at the office. Afterwards, we all went to our own little corners.

At my desk, I stared at my ten vocabulary words. The shortest story I could think of was, "There once was a girl named Jannette. She had to learn and memorize ten vocabulary words. The words were fractiousness, accentuated, infinitesimal, cordial, rivulets, somnambulatory, caravansary, vicariously, portentous, and bulbous. Using flash cards, she was able to memorize them in record time. The end." Here's hoping Mr. Warren won't make me do it again. I set that aside and started researching Hawaii. Maka did say I could ask him if I had any questions. Eve offered to help countless times. She even gave me her cell number.

I found a flower that caught my eye. Almost breath-taking. A bright blue indigenous flower called *Morning Glory*. I figured those could be the pawns on one side of the chess board and my first drawing as well. Well, my attempt of a drawing, anyway. Drawing in a sketchbook my mom bought me, I drew about nine of those flowers. I read online that the flower can be found mostly by beaches.

Finding It

So, I drew a beach with waves coming in from the ocean. It didn't look too bad. But the coloring would either make this or break it. I decided to leave well enough alone and pick it up again tomorrow.

I finished the rest of my homework and packed all my field hockey gear. I couldn't be any more excited for tryouts tomorrow. After my shower, the clock read nearly ten o'clock. I climbed into bed and looked up at the ceiling, thinking about what Eve had said at lunch. The way she put everything made it easy to understand her point of view. But the whole God thing was... I don't know. I was just glad she didn't press me about the subject afterwards. I had no doubt it would come up again. But until then, I needed some rest. Tomorrow would be great.

3

I woke up this morning with a smile. I got dressed, still smiling. I brushed my teeth with a smile. Surprisingly enough, I still had a smile in English class. Eve asked me what was up. So, I showed her how I'd completed my vocabulary homework. She laughed. I turned the paper in, laying it on Mr. Warren's desk.

As I sat next to Eve, I said, "I really hope he takes my story. I really don't want to do it again."

"I don't know," she replied. "He doesn't seem to be the type to joke around like that."

"He can't say too much about it. I did follow directions." I paused and thought. "Right?"

"Well, you did follow directions," she said apprehensively. "I think he's looking at it right now."

We both watched Mr. Warren to see if any expression came across his face. Once the rest of the class come in, we lost sight of Mr. Warren. When my line of sight improved, he was looking straight at me. I looked down at my desk so quickly I couldn't tell if he was angry or not.

"Good morning, class. Has anyone else finished their vocabulary homework?"

The vocabulary homework wasn't due until tomorrow, so no one raised their hand. I held my breath.

"Well, I have an interesting story here. It's creative and followed the directions. It reads..."

The students laughed along with Mr. Warren. He walked over to my desk and handed me the paper. I looked at it and, on top, it had one-hundred written in red. "Ms. Sentmore, next time I would like a slightly longer story with context clues. Maybe some definition in both aspects of the word. As funny as this was, you won't get that kind of grade for this kind of work again. Understood?"

"Yes, sir."

At the end of class, the bell rang and Eve followed me to my locker. "I still can't believe he gave you a one-hundred."

"Honestly, neither can I. I thought he was going to make me do it over."

"Are you ready for this afternoon?"

"Oh yeah." I showed her my field hockey bag.

"I really hope I make it this year," Eve said.

"Really quick—where is the music room?"

"Across the hall from my calculus class."

"Cool, show me." I closed my locker door. "What position are you wanting?"

"Well, running wasn't my strongest point at camp. They always played me sweeper or goalie."

"Which one do you think you're strongest in?"

"Goalie," she said without hesitation.

"Then try out as goalie. You want them to see you at your strongest. When you make the team, let the coach try you in other positions. You want to be confident." My advice sounded more like an order than advice.

"Never thought of it that way," Eve said. "How long have you been playing?"

"I started playing in the sixth grade. I loved it then and still love it now."

"That's Ms. Colner's music room." Eve pointed to a classroom across the way. "This is me. Are you going to be eating with us again today?"

Not that I had much of a choice. "Sure."

"Great, I'll see you then."

I walked into the classroom and there were old-fashioned desks. Ones that had the desk attached to the chairs. The desks sat on what looked like wide steps that a choir would stand on for a concert. I saw Ms. Colner, a hefty woman with shiny red hair. She looked like she should be singing in an opera.

Ms. Colner asked what we thought we would accomplish in her music class this year. When she went over the curriculum, I was intrigued for a minute or two. Essentially, we were going to learn about music from around the world, the history behind the music and which cultural instruments were used. I could tell that the students were giving the teacher answers that any teacher would want to hear. I always hated when people lie. I was going to answer honestly. I doubted she would like what I had to say.

"Ms. Leona Sentmore, what do you think you are going to accomplish in my music class this year?"

"May I speak honestly?"

"Of course," she said, a puzzled tone colored her voice.

I took a deep breath and let it out slowly. "I don't think I'm going to accomplish much in this class other than an easy A and a higher GPA." Some of the students turned in their seats, looking at me, wide-eyed.

Ms. Colner sucked in her breath and held it. Although she hid it well, behind that tranquil face I could tell I'd struck a nerve.

I decided it was probably best to clarify my point of view. "What you hope that we get from your class is a greater appreciation for a wide variety of music. But for the most part, we already like the kind of music that we like. People who end up with an eclectic taste in music can end up on the streets begging for money. Or as teacher, not making much at all."

After a moment, Ms. Cloner finally asked, "What about the people that have made millions from the music they make?"

"They normally make that money with one genre of music. When did Elvis Presley make anything other than rock and roll? Michael Jackson only sang pop. Mozart, nothing other than classical. I'll learn from what you show me of music around the world, but to gain anything from it? I just don't see me gaining anything more from music than what I already have."

"Does anyone agree with Ms. Sentmore?" She looked around the room and no one raised their hand. "Okay. Well, Leona, see me after class."

I had dug myself a giant hole.

The bell rang and everyone headed for the door. I moved from the back row to the front and waited. Whatever she was going to say, I wasn't going to like it. Ms. Colner closed the door and I saw Eve's head pop up through the window in the door. I signaled to her to go on ahead.

Ms. Colner cleared her throat. "Leona, I can appreciate your honesty."

That was a lie.

"I'm sure you are not the only one who thinks that way. You're just the only one who has ever said it."

"I meant no disrespect, Ms. Colner. I just wanted to be honest with my opinion."

"Yes... and now I am going to be truthful with you. If you deserve an A, you will get and A. If you deserve a B then you will get a B. But your assignments will differ from everyone else's. That way your grade won't be so..." She looked me square in the eye. "*Easy.* I am determined to change your mind. That's my goal."

Good luck, I thought to myself. She dismissed me and went to the cafeteria. I grabbed my lunch and took a seat next to Eve. I hadn't even sat down and she was talking.

"Why were you held after class?"

I told her what happened. Maka and his friends tuned into the conversation. As I get deeper into the story, a guy named Mark stopped eating. With his mouth open and full of food, he stared at me with the same rounded eyes as the other students had.

Eve said, "Oh my goodness. I can't believe you said that."

"She wanted the truth and I gave it to her. It's not my fault she couldn't handle it."

"With that attitude you could be a great pastor." That was an unexpected comment, coming from Maka. "Some pastors are afraid of speaking the truth because of how it may settle with the congregation."

I gave Maka the dirtiest look I can muster up. "Pastoring is not my thing."

He chuckled and, with his hands up as if I were holding a gun to him, he said, "Okay. It's not your thing." He smiled and went back to eating.

"How did you do that?" Eve asked with a tone of amazement.

"Do what?"

"Get my brother to shut up like that." Maka threw a napkin at her. She laughed. "I do think what you said to Ms. Colner, although true, was disrespectful. But it did take some courage to speak your mind like that. I'm sure there is a balance to be found for that."

"You lost me... a balance for what?"

"A balance for being truthful, courageous, and still respectful."

"If I have an opinion, why should I express it in anyway other than how it comes to mind?"

"Because your opinion is worth listening to."

I gave her a confused look.

She took a breath. "If you state your point of view disrespectfully, no one is going to listen. People will think you're rude and write off what you've said. Say it respectfully and people may actually consider what you say."

I had no rebuttal, so I nodded and kept eating.

In my last class, I sat next to Eve. Normally, Ms. Wells' class was interesting, but my mind was out in left field. I'd end up doing my classwork for homework.

"Are you okay?" Eve whispered.

"Yeah, my mind is just thinking about this afternoon."

"What if you don't even make the team?"

"I will. And if I can help it, so will you."

"How do you know?" She stopped working and stared at me.

"I just know."

She smiled and said, "You're confident as well. Courageous and confident, two very good traits to have."

After a moment of eye contact, I got back to work.

Why do I get the feeling that she knows something that I don't? Every time she says something, she was always upbeat and sure about what she said. She seemed sincere... but I just didn't trust her yet. I didn't know why.

Anyway, I attempted to finish my classwork. Surprisingly, I handed in my paper just as the bell rang. Eve and I walked to our lockers and collected our gear. Leland said he would text me when tryouts were over for him, and we'd meet up at the car. We got dressed in the locker room.

The goalie for field hockey most resembled a goalie for ice hockey. Only our goalie wore cleats instead of ice skates. I helped Eve bring all her gear out to the field. We gathered on the bleachers and waited to hear the coaches speak. In the meantime, I counted heads. There were thirty-six girls going out for the team, but only twenty-two positions open. Fourteen of these girls won't make the team. Eight more people and they would have had enough to make both a JV and a varsity with no cuts.

"Good afternoon, ladies." The chatter quieted. "For those of you who don't already know, my name is Coach Conner. New to our team is Assistant Coach Ash." Everyone applauded. "Like myself, Coach Ash was offered an opportunity to try out for the Olympic field hockey team. Also like me, she got injured and didn't make the cut." Coach Conner turned back to us. "Okay, so this year's tryouts are going to be slightly different. First, if you were on the team last year, you are not guaranteed a slot on the team this year. Even if you were a captain or a starter. There are three afternoon tryouts. At the end of today, we will call out two lists of names. If your name is called out in the first list of names, then you didn't make the team this year. If your name is called out in the second list, then you'll need to come tomorrow, ready to impress. You are still at risk of being cut. Tomorrow, we will make the final decision for the twenty-two players. For those of you who make the team, Thursday is tryouts for positions and starter slots. We will also select this year's captains. That is the only time we expect you ladies to compete against each other. Before you warm up, come and see us. We have your last names written on Scotch tape. This will help us identify each of you. When you have your names, run two laps around the field and stretch out."

You could tell who'd kept in shape during the off-season. I finished my laps fourth. I walked over to Eve and told her to cover a goal while I practiced shots. I saw why Eve didn't make the team last year. She missed any shots above her knees. She didn't seem too keen on using her padded hand to protect the goal. Almost like she was afraid of getting hurt by the ball. I went to tell her, but the coaches called and split us up.

There were two groups. We ran drills, practiced penalty shots, and sprints. When time was up, the coaches told everyone to sit on the bleachers. While they spoke with their backs to us, I noticed Coach Ash pointed and gestured a lot. Both women turned and walked toward us, stopping just a few feet short of the bleachers.

Coach Conner was the one who spoke. "First, we want to thank everyone for coming out today. But not everyone can make the team. For those of you who didn't, please know that Coach Ash and I have a field hockey training camp over the winter and summer. If you would like to join, please see one of us. We apologize, but the following people didn't make the first cut..." She named six people. "The following thirteen people will have to come tomorrow and do some convincing." Eve was the seventh name they called. They didn't call my name. "Again, sorry to those who didn't make it this year. For the rest of you, we will see you tomorrow."

I didn't hesitate. "Okay, Eve, you are coming to my house. We are sharpening up your goalie skills."

"I'm not allowed to go over anyone's house during the week. Unless it's for a school project. But you can come to my house."

I don't know why, but being invited to her house was something I hadn't expected. "Fine, I'll call my mother."

We walked to the locker room. When we got there, we both called home. "Hey, Mom, can I go to Eve's house tonight?"

"Who is Eve?" She sounded preoccupied.

"A friend from school. Can I go?" Just then Eve turned to me and gave me a thumbs up.

"Text me another number I can reach you at. Preferably a parent's number."

I looked at Eve. "She wants your mother's number."

Eve took the phone. "Mrs. Sentmore? My name is Eve. Would you happen to have a pen to write down my mother's number?" She rattled it off. "Yes ma'am. We will do our homework, eat dinner, and practice. Yes ma'am. No, my brother and I can bring her home. Okay. Well you have a blessed evening." She handed me the phone.

"Can I go?" I asked, just to be sure.

"Yes, call me if anything changes."

"Yup, bye." I texted Leland and let him know my plans.

We met up with Maka, who drove us to their home. As we approached the door, Eve warned me. "Okay, my mom loves having people over. She'll give you a hug and a kiss. She'll try and help you with your homework while cooking. Then she'll feed you until you can't move."

I chuckled. "Sounds like my kind of woman."

We dropped our bags when Eve's mom came around the corner. "Did you two have a good day at school?" She gave them both a hug and a kiss on the cheek. The top of her head fell just short of

Maka's chin. She had the same caramel skin and the same jet black hair as Maka and Eve. Her eyes were not as Asian-looking as theirs, though. She wore a bright green flowery skirt with a solid green shirt. She looked at me with a big smile. "You must be Leona. It's very nice to meet you."

I smiled back. She gave me a tight hug and a kiss on the cheek. I glanced over at Eve and she shot me a look that said, "See?"

"Do you have any food allergies, Leona?"

"No, I'm a human dumpster. I'll eat anything." I took a breath and realized what I said. I quickly corrected. "Except trash."

She giggled. "Well, I'm glad to meet you. We'll talk more over dinner. But now, it's time for homework."

Their house was much bigger than it looked from the outside. Eve and I put all of our belongings in her room. We made our way to the dining room table with our homework. We started working and Mrs. Aquino would periodically stop cooking and ask if we needed help. Eve and I worked together and read for the classes that we shared.

Maka sat across the table from me. He said that he could help me with anything I might need. This family seemed to want to help, a little too much. I'd never heard of anyone wanting to help this much. I figured I would hold off coloring my drawings until Friday. I had until the last bell on Friday to turn in my work.

This drawing was of a flower called *Wax Vine*. It's a light pink flower with a magenta center. I drew the vine going across the top of the page with three clusters falling from the vine. But what I drew only covered a third of the page. I flipped between the only two drawings I'd done, trying to figure out what I could do for the rest of the page. From behind me, Mrs. Aquino said, "Oh, that's the Wax Vine and that would be Morning Glory, yes?"

I turned to face her. "Yes."

She pulled up a chair. "May I suggest something?"

"Sure."

"Many times, in Hawaii, I see this flower around the trunk of a tree or with the support of a fence. But my favorite flower was always the Lilikoi."

I wrote the name down. "Where you born in Hawaii, Mrs. Aquino?"

She shook her head. "No, I was born on Upolu Island, in Samoa. I moved to Hawaii when I was a girl."

I'd thought the Samoan Islands *were* the Hawaiian Islands. "May I ask you a question? It could help spark some ideas for next week." She nodded, smiling. "What is something that you miss? Something you don't see as often anymore."

Without hesitation she said, "My culture."

"What do you mean by *your culture*?"

"You see, my culture is becoming scarce. In Vermont, next to us three, you don't see many of my people. We are much more common in Hawaii. Even in Hawaii, my people are very proud. But the culture and traditions over the years are slowly being lost. Something like the American Indians' cultures." She paused. She walked over to the kitchen, stirred a few things and returned to her seat. "The American Indians have been pushed out and away by various things. There is a small amount of them who still practice their original traditions and speak their original language. It slowly is dissipating." She looked around and asked, "Is everyone finished with their homework?"

When we all nodded *yes*, she said, "Okay, then. Let's eat."

Mrs. Aquino served everyone angel hair pasta with chicken and sauce. A bowl of green salad with diced cucumber, mint leaves, and carrots sat on the table. I was going for my fork until Eve and Mrs. Aquino each took one of my hands to pray. Maka said grace. I felt so awkward that I forgot to bow my head.

When we released hands, Maka said, "To best experience this dish, just make a mess." He took the sauce, poured it over his food and mixed everything together.

I followed his example and it was delicious. "Mrs. Aquino, may I ask you some more questions?"

"Of course."

"You said that your culture and tradition are slowly being lost. Is there anything specific you meant by that?"

She finished chewing and swallowed. "Tataus."

"Ta... what?"

"Tatau. They are something like tattoos. In my culture, between the ages of fifteen and twenty, people get Tataus. It's like today's tattoos, but instead of a needle machine, we use bamboo and tortoise shell. The men get their whole body done if they want. Women usually just do their legs. Tattoos are common now, but they aren't the same."

"Did you get your tatau?"

She smiled and shifted in her seat. She extended her legs to the side of the table so that I could see. She lifted her skirt halfway up her thighs. "Of course, I did. I got it done when I was nineteen." It was a series of lines and triangles, creating a pattern that formed diamonds. It went from just below her knee, to further than her skirt revealed.

Still staring, I said, "That's beautiful. Does it go all the way around your legs?" She'd returned eating and so she nodded.

"Wow. And you said that men get more than that done?"

"Right. Sometimes when the men get it done, it takes days to finish. Depending on what they get, it could take weeks."

"Do you have one?" I asked Eve.

"No, and I don't plan on getting one," she answered.

"Why?"

"Because I think it's defiling God's temple."

Mrs. Aquino said something I didn't understand. She had a pensive look on her face. "I tell you what. If your parents say it's all right and pay for the plane ticket, we could take you to Hawaii with us in November. We can show you tataus, the instruments, everything."

"How much is the plane ticket?"

"About fifteen-hundred. I'll write down all the information and give it to you before you leave."

I thought for a moment, then said, "Count me in."

Eve chimed in. "But you haven't even asked your parents yet."

"Oh, I am *so* going."

When we'd finished eating, Maka and Eve cleaned up. Mrs. Aquino and I spoke more about tataus and the process of it.

All four of us went to their fenced-in back yard to help Eve with practice. The field hockey ball was the size a softball, but as hard as a golf ball. Fear of the ball was common when people were new to the sport. But Eve had a helmet with a caged mask and a butt-load of padding. I took a ball and threw it at her. It hit her at the top of her helmet. Maka laughed. While her attention was on Maka, who was still laughing, I grabbed my other ball and threw it at her. This time it hit her in the cage of the mask. She turned and, with an aggravated tone, she asked, "Leona, what are you doing?"

I apologized. "I'm sorry, Eve, but you are the goalie and the ball is your enemy. You can't fear the ball. You can't wait for the ball to come to you, sometimes you have to go after it. Now we're going to go through few drills and I want you to be aggressive. Remember, there aren't many rules for you while protecting the goal. If you want to dive or slide to protect the goal, do it. Got it?"

She smiled. "Got it."

We practiced for an hour and a half before wrapping things up. "Eve, you're going to do great tomorrow." I honestly thought so.

Mrs. Aquino said, "You did great, Kai. Leona, are you comfortable with Makaio taking you home?"

I nodded and shrugged at the same time.

"Kai, you have chores to do." Mrs. Aquino handed me an index card with the information for the trip. We would leave early on November twenty-first, returning December first. She wrote her name, *Moana Aquino,* with the address and phone number of their house in Kauai.

In the car, Maka and I spoke about a few things. He said he wasn't into church the way his mom and sister were but that he believed firmly in the Bible and its teachings. He said he was a leader in the church until his father passed. I felt bad, so I stopped talking. When we got to my house, Maka helped me with my bags and walked me to the door. Once inside, Mother asked me about my afternoon. I told her about everything... but the trip to Hawaii. I had to be careful about how to approach that one. I took a shower and went straight to bed. While lying in bed, I thought of ways to convince my parents to let me go to Hawaii. I fell asleep with nothing solid.

4

I woke up still thinking about Hawaii. While I brushed my teeth, I thought of something. *My account.* My parents had set up an account for each of their kids when we were born. They put in a dollar for every day we stayed away from cigarettes, drugs, and alcohol. The savings couldn't be touched until we brought home our high school diploma. But, the checking account, where they put all the money that we got for our birthdays and allowances... we were allowed discretion with our checking account money.

After our tenth birthday, our parents had given us a choice. We could put the money into our accounts or spend it. Our allowance was ten dollars a week, which doesn't sound like much, but for someone like me, who rarely spent money, it's added up. I ran to my computer to check my account. I had three-thousand and thirty-six dollars.

I couldn't buy the ticket now because my parents held onto the debit cards. I guess it was just their way of helping us build good saving and spending habits. I grabbed my backpack and field hockey bag and ran out to the car. I realized that Leland hadn't brought his bag. "Lee, where is your gym bag?"

"I didn't make the team."

"What? Why?"

He shrugged. "I'm gonna to have to figure out a way to stay in shape before I enlist."

"Have you chosen a branch?"

"I think probably the Marines."

"Well, maybe I could talk to Maka. He goes to a gym that competes in mixed martial arts. Maybe you can check it out."

"Can you talk to him today?"

I nodded.

"Cool."

After a minute, I asked, "Lee, do you think Mom and Dad would let me use my money to buy a ticket to go to Hawaii?"

"Hawaii? Why Hawaii?"

"I have Hawaii for my place of origin in art class. Eve's family is from Hawaii. They are going for a little over a week in November. Her mom said that if we buy the plane ticket and if Mom and Dad say it's okay... I can go with them."

"How much is the ticket?"

"About fifteen-hundred. More if you wait too long."

"How much do you have in your account?"

"Just over three-grand."

"Jeeezzzz... I only have like eight-hundred dollars. Let me borrow some money," he said playfully.

"Focus Leland, *Hawaii.*"

He chuckled. "Honestly, I don't know. They've never turned me down for anything I've asked for. But I never asked for anything that big."

"You bought your drum set."

"Yes, but I didn't have to leave the country to get it."

"Neither will I." I paused then whispered, "*Technically.*"

"I think your best bet is to just come out and ask them. Give them all the information and hope for the best."

"I was wishing for something better than that." I jabbed him in the ribs.

Finding It

. . .

AT THE END of Mr. Warren's class, Ms. Lumina came in.

Facepalm. I completely forgot.

She walked over to Mr. Warren's desk. On the way, using sign language, she signed, "We will leave together."

I whispered to Eve that I'd meet up with her at lunch. The bell rang and Ms. Lumina and I walked out together.

"Leona, I have spoken to all your teachers."

I raised an eyebrow, waiting. I pressed my lips together and nodded. Whatever Ms. Lumina hoped to accomplish with this little meeting, so far, it's only made me uncomfortable.

I was ushered into her fairly small office.

"Your parents mentioned that you know American Sign Language. Do you mind if I ask how you learned signing?" She closed the door behind us.

I sat down. "How did that come up?"

She took a piece of paper and sat down in front of me. With her voice soft and steady she said, "They were using the fact that you'd learned American Sign Language faster than anyone in the family as an example of how smart you are."

I didn't know how smart you had to be to learn sign language. The hardest part was keeping up with the people who've been signing their whole lives. They sign faster than we talk. "One of my aunts on my dad's side was in the military. We took care of her son, who is deaf. She was deployed overseas. She ended up passing away during her second tour. He stayed with us a total of four years. He moved out on his own when I was in the eighth grade."

"Do you still talk to him?"

"I Skype with him from time to time."

"That's good." She paused, looking down at the paper. After a moment, she looked at me and said, "So, like I said before... I spoke with all of your teachers. For the most part, everything came back good."

"I should hope so, it's only been three days."

"Do you want to tell me about your encounter with Ms. Colner?"

I sighed and rolled my eyes. I'd forgotten about that already. As I contemplated what to tell her, she spoke.

"You don't have to tell me. But I will say this; I am the one who decides on whether this continues after the holidays. As of right now I have nothing good to say about music class unless you tell me your side of the story."

"What is there to tell? She asked for my opinion and I gave it to her. *Honestly.*" People made it sound like it was the end of the world.

"Do you remember what you said?"

"No... not exactly." If I knew I was going to get quizzed, I would have written it down. "Something like I didn't think I was going to accomplish much. Other than an easy A and a higher GPA."

"So, you said her class was *worthless*?" Her voice didn't fluctuate. At all.

"Well if you want to put it viciously."

"You don't think what you said was vicious or disrespectful?"

"I asked if I could be honest and she said *yes*. When has anyone ever started a conversation like that and said something positive? Ms. Colner said that she set a goal to change my mind. If by chance she ends up changing my mind then I will openly admit that I was wrong. But until then, I stand by what I said."

"Okay, I am going to ask you two more questions on this subject. Afterwards, we will move on until another day."

I sat back and folded my arms, preparing for her questions.

"Have you ever been called worthless?"

I hesitated to answer. "Yes, actually I have." *More times than I would like to count.*

"What did you do about it?"

"The same thing Ms. Colner is doing. I set out to change their mind."

"Right. Let's now talk about something you enjoy. How is field hockey going?"

"I made the team," I said, trying to hide my excitement.

"I thought tryouts weren't until Thursday."

"They called six names of people who'd been cut yesterday. They called another eight of people who were at risk of being cut. They never called my name. So, I made the team."

We chatted until I was surprised to hear the bell ring, what seemed only minutes later.

I made it to the cafeteria, got some lunch, and sat with the usual bunch.

Eve asked, "Can I ask what that was about?"

"What? Ms. Lumina?" She nodded. "I dug myself into a hole last year. I have to talk to her every other week because of it."

"Can I ask about... last year?"

"I'd rather you didn't." I shifted to turn toward Maka. "Maka, my brother Leland didn't make the football team. He wants to find a way to stay in shape. I told him about your gym. Do you think he can check it out some time?"

"Definitely, when does he want to come by?" he said, still chewing.

"Can I just give you his number and you two work out the details? It would be simpler."

"Sure, what's his number?" We both pulled out our cell phones and exchanged numbers.

The rest of the day went smoothly. Eve and I were in the locker room getting ready for tryouts. As we walk out to the field, I felt nervous. "How are you feeling?"

"I feel good." Again, very upbeat.

"Remember, the ball is your enemy. Be aggressive."

She smiled. "Yup."

Tryouts today were about the same as yesterday. We scrimmaged against each other. I found out that there was already a goalie who'd made the team. Eve was competing for the second slot. I really hoped she makes it. While we waited on the bleachers for the coaches to finish up, they stood with their backs to us. My nerves were on edge.

Watching Coach Conner and Coach Ash, I noticed that Ash was signing. They finally turned around and Coach Conner was the one who spoke. "Okay, so for those of you don't make the team, we will be holding training camp this winter. I apologize, but the following people didn't make the team." She named eight names while I held my breath. They got to the end of the list without calling Eve's name.

I looked over at Eve. She was smiling from ear to ear. "For the twenty-two that made it, congratulations. We will see you tomorrow."

The whole way to the locker room, Eve kept thanking me. All the way to the parking lot, I heard, "I can't thank you enough." She got so excited her voice would occasionally squeak. I couldn't help but laugh. I spotted Leland and Maka talking—both with their shirts off. When we got close enough, Eve shouted, "Guess what? I made the team!"

Maka smiled and said, "Nice."

"Good job," Leland said.

"Those two balls you threw at her head did the trick, didn't it, Leona?" Maka said.

I rolled my eyes.

"Yes, they did," Eve admitted.

I looked at Leland. "Did you go to the gym already?"

"Yup. I'm going to start training there. It's only seventy-five dollars a month. I can handle that until the end of the year. I just have to let Mom and Dad know."

"Don't tell them until I get to ask if I can go to Hawaii."

"You haven't asked them yet?" Eve asked.

I shook my head. "It's not the best idea on wait on that," Maka said. "Those tickets can get up to four-grand, if you wait long enough."

"I have the money. I just need to get them to let me use it for the trip. I'll talk to them tonight."

"Let me know when you drop your bomb—that way mine won't look so bad," Leland joked.

"Yeah, until you tell them you're joining the military."

Leland pushed me. "Touché."

"My father was in the military," Eve chimed in. "What branch are you joining?"

"The Marines."

"Dad was a firefighter in the Marines," Maka said, looking at the ground.

"Your dad was an American?" I thought they had Asian in them, so it left me thoroughly confused.

Maka nodded. "On paper."

Eve saw the confused look on my face. "Dad was born in the Philippines, then moved to Texas when he was a boy. He joined the military when he was old enough and got stationed in Hawaii, where he met and married Mom. After four years in Hawaii, he reenlisted and was stationed here in Vermont. When he retired, he moved back to Hawaii and had us. You know the story from there on."

"Oh. I get it." It was time to head home. "I'll call you when I can get the tickets, okay?"

When I got home, I didn't wait. I went straight to the kitchen where I knew mom would be. "Hey Mom, where is Dad? I kind of wanted to talk to you both about something."

"He's working late tonight, honey." She didn't even look up. "But he is taking the day off tomorrow... you can talk to us then. Can it wait?"

"Sure."

I went to my room, did my homework, and took a bath. When I finished, Leland was on my bed. I jumped on him and asked, "What are you doing on my bed?"

"I just signed up to take a test with the Marines. I'm taking it first thing Friday morning."

"Don't you need Mom and Dad's permission? You're only seventeen."

"Not to take the test. If I was enlisting, yes." He paused. "I'm going to wait until I turn eighteen to enlist. That way I won't need their permission." He got up. "You think you can catch a ride to school Monday? That way I can head straight to the recruiting office."

"I think so."

"If not, let me know. I can reschedule."

"Okay." He left and I crawled under the covers. My brother, *the Marine*. It had a ring to it. Now that he figured out what he would do after high school, it was probably best for me to figure out what I wanted to do. I'd start brainstorming tomorrow.

5

When I woke in the morning, I heard Mom and Dad talking in the kitchen. I didn't wait. I grabbed the information and ran for the kitchen. "Mom, Dad can I talk to you about something?"

Mother didn't even look up but I heard her sigh. My father set his coffee cup down. Smiling, he said, "Good morning, Leona. How have you been? Wow, you've grown."

His sarcasm was over the top today.

I rolled my eyes, but grinned. "Good morning, Daddy." I leaned in and gave him a hug. "How has work been?"

"Work is work. Now, tell us what's on your mind."

I briefly glanced at each of them. Mom was cutting her fried eggs, but Dad gave me his attention. I inhaled. "I was hoping you guys would let me use the money in my account for a trip to Hawaii."

Dad's eyebrows hit his hairline and Mom looked up, wide eyed. I defensively shot out my hands in front of me, palms out. "Okay, let me explain. In art class, we have what we call a *place of origin*. A place that we have to research and get our inspiration from to create homework. I got Hawaii. Turns out that girl, Eve, and her family are from Hawaii. Well, they're going in November for a week... well, ten days. Mrs. Aquino said that if you say it's okay, and we pay for my plane ticket, that I can go with them." I'd started talking faster. I set the index card on the table. "Here, Mrs. Aquino even wrote all the information down."

Dad looked it over. Mom's eyebrows were furrowed in concentration. Or annoyance. My eyes bounced back and forth between them.

Dad took a long, slow drink of coffee, then calmly asked, "You can take a trip to Hawaii any time you want. Why now? Other than you wouldn't have to pay hotel expenses by going with your friend."

"Well, I will only have Hawaii for my place of origin until January. The teacher offers a perfect grade for the whole semester to whoever can surprise him with their artwork. In order to do that I need to *know* Hawaii. I need to *go to Hawaii*. Now that the opportunity is right in front of me, I want to take it."

Dad still fished for more information. "How much is the ticket?"

"Right now, about fifteen-hundred. The longer we wait, the more expensive it gets."

"How much do you have in your account?"

"Just over three-grand."

"I assume you would want your debit card for the trip as well?"

I nodded. My father inhaled deeply and nodded once. "Well, your mother and I will need to discuss this. Go get ready for school. We'll let you know when we have made a decision."

"Okay... thanks." I left the room. Well, as far as around the corner where I stopped. I wanted to hear their reactions.

"What do you think?" Dad asked.

"I don't think we should let her go."

Of course, my mother would be against it.

"I think we should."

"You can't be serious."

There was a pause.

"You think we should let her go to Hawaii with people we don't even know? Hell, Lucas, she can't know them that well—she's

Finding It

known Eve four days!" Mom's voice got louder the longer she talked.

I hated to admit it, but my mother had a good point.

"If it were Logan or Leland, we would have said *yes* by now. I don't even think we would have discussed it."

"Logan and Leland have never given us the same problems Leona has."

I clenched my fists, wishing she would just let that go already.

"So? She's made a few mistakes."

"A *year's* worth of mistakes, Lucas." You could tell my mother was irritated the way she said *Lucas*.

"I still think she has a reason for last year." There was another pause, then Dad continued. "But you can't expect her to move past that if you keep bringing it up."

"I know... I know. It's just after last year, I half expect her to fail again."

What?

"Wow, Lillian. That's probably one of the worst things you could have said about our daughter."

Yeah, tell me what you really think, Mom.

Dad broke the silence. "I don't think a trip to Hawaii would destroy her life. We'll just give that *Moana* lady a call today. Ask her questions, get to know her and we'll go from there."

I'd heard enough. As I got ready for school, I thought about what my mother said. She figured I was going to fail. She made it sound like I was the evil seed of *Chucky* next to Logan and Leland. She must have stuck her head in the sand if she honestly thought Leland had never smoked a cigarette. I'd caught him smoking last year. Or that Logan didn't drink during his freshmen year in college. He called me, drunk, four times that year. I'd found Logan's dirty DVD stash in the fifth grade.

I was probably more of a saint than either of them. I finished getting ready and quietly walked to the living room. I listened to hear if my parents were still discussing me.

Father was talking. "Can't be that bad if he's joining a gym with Eve's brother." *Huh, so they have spoken to Leland.*

"But he said the family is religious. We have never discussed religion in this house."

I sighed. *Bring down the drama a few notches, will ya, Mom?*

"Would her inheriting this religious thing from her friend really be that bad? It could be what she needs to get on track. It's not like she talks to us."

My mother sounding irritated. "Why do you defend her so much?"

My father matched her irritation. "Because you won't."

Someone took a deep breath and exhaled loudly.

"Lillian," Dad said, in a much calmer tone. "Leona isn't a straight-A student, but she isn't a drug addict, either. I think if we let her go on this trip, she'll find what she needs to get that perfect grade. It might even inspire her to do better in her other classes."

I was done listening. I walked into the kitchen. "So, what's the verdict?"

They looked at each other.

Mom spoke up. "I'm going to call Moana today and talk to her. Get to know her a bit and... we'll see. Okay, sweetie?"

Oh, so now you thought I was a sweetie. Just a minute ago, I was your failure. "Okay."

Leland came around the corner. "Let's go, squirt."

"What's with you?" Leland asked, once outside.

"I asked Mom and Dad about Hawaii." I buckled my seatbelt.

"Yeah, they asked me what I knew about the family. I did get the okay about the gym. Thanks for that."

"No problem," I said, staring out the window.

"Well? What happened?"

"I listened in and Mom brought up last year *again*. I don't know." I sighed. "She makes it sound like I'll never live it down."

"You will. I'll even give you permission to flip her the bird when you show her your diploma."

I punched his arm playfully.

As I walked from English to music with Eve, she asked, "Everything okay today? You seem a little off."

I shrugged. "I spoke to my parents this morning about Hawaii. I don't know. Mom wasn't happy about it. Dad doesn't mind. They said they would call your mom for more information."

"Didn't my mother write down the information for you?"

"Yes, and I gave it to them. I don't know what they're looking for, but they said they'd call... hey, can I ask you something?"

"Sure."

"Have you had Ms. Colner before?" She nodded. "Any advice on how to deal with her?"

"Just do what she asks you to." She stopped at her classroom door. "Saying what you did the other day... I think landed you on an iceberg. You might not have much choice but to float to where it takes you."

When I walked in, Ms. Colner took some papers from the top of the piano and handed them to me. I stood there, expecting her to hand me the same assignment as everyone else. I realized mine was different. I was to listen to how these instruments were used in African music. After I'd listened to the music, she instructed me to write a paragraph or two on how it made me feel. *Awesome.*

As I walked out of the classroom, Ms. Colner called to me. "Leona." I looked her way. "That will be your homework assignment all year."

I furrowed my eyebrows. "Yes ma'am."

In the cafeteria, I got something to eat. More out of habit, because my appetite was absent.

"Leona?" Eve snapped her fingers. "Leona, you haven't eaten anything, are you okay?"

"It's just one thing."

"Seems like a big *one thing*. Do you want to talk about?"

I felt mischievous. "I'm pregnant." Her eyes widened, she

gasped, and her mouth dropped open. I tried to keep a straight face, but I couldn't. Giggling, I said, "I'm just kidding."

"Oh," she said with relief.

"I wish I had a picture of your face." I chuckled.

"So, do you want to talk about the *real* problem?"

"I know you only want to help." I changed the subject. "Would you mind spotting me for a ride to school tomorrow?"

She tapped Maka on the shoulder. "Can we give Leona a ride to school tomorrow morning?"

"Sure. What's up?"

"Leland is taking his military test first thing."

"Oh, sweet," Maka said. "See you in the morning." He turned back to his friends.

WE SCRIMMAGED ALL PRACTICE. The coaches tried everyone in different positions. They even tried me as goalie. When time was up, Coach Conner said that the results would be posted on the door of their office tomorrow morning. As long as I made the team, who cared what position I played?

When we got home, Mom and Dad were in the living room. Before I even had a chance to ask, my mother announced, "Leland, Leona, we will be eating dinner with the Aquino family Sunday night."

Later, I sat at my desk trying to finish my homework. I had my sketch pad, but the only thing I could think of was what my mother said this morning. I don't know why it still bothered me so much.

I took a shower and went to bed, still dwelling on my mom's words.

I wasn't mad, I felt hurt.

6

I woke up without any desire to get out of bed. Leland and I met up with Maka and Eve. Leland went to take his test. The rest of us headed to school. Standing at my locker, I heard someone call my name. Eve rushed up to me.

"I don't have much time," she said, slightly out of breath. "But I wanted to be the first to say, *congratulations!*" She leaped forward and hugged me. "Gotta go, I'll see you in English."

In Spanish class, I tried to figure out what Eve had congratulated me for.

Back at my locker after Spanish, I heard a voice.

"I am impressed." I looked around and saw the boy from the pizza diner, Rodney. He leaned on the locker next to mine.

"Impressed about what?" I kept shuffling my books to get ready for the next class.

"I figured with the confidence you showed that you would make the team. I never thought you'd be a starter..."

I stopped listening.

"Let alone landing *co-captain*," he finished.

I closed my locker door. "I told you I would make the team."

"That you did." He shifted his locker-leaning-position to face me. "Maybe us two C.C.s should get together for dinner tomorrow night. What do you say?"

I think he just asked me out. "What?"

"Dinner and a movie. You and me. *Tomorrow*," he said.

I didn't know what to say. I'd never been asked out before.

"Are you allowed to date?"

"Ummm… yeah." *I think.* "Tomorrow sounds great."

"Great. I'll pick you up around seven tomorrow night. Here's my number." He hands me a piece of ripped binder paper. "Text me tonight so we can plan the rest of the details."

Details? "Okay."

I texted Rodney while walking to English.

Eve sat next to me. "I can't believe you're so calm about this."

"Calm about what?" I'm beginning to get frustrated.

"Didn't you go check the postings for the field hockey positions this morning?"

"No."

"Well you should know that you got co-captain," she said with attitude in her tone.

"What?" I stared at Eve, who gave me a huge smile.

"You're co-captain, Leona."

I don't know what to think. "I got co-captain?"

Just when I thought Eve's smile couldn't get any bigger. "Yes!"

Mr. Warren called for the class's attention.

I looked forward and said, "Snap."

"Hey, are we still practicing tomorrow?"

"Yeah, sure. What time?"

"Well, if you come over at about eleven-thirty in the morning you can have lunch with me and my family. Then we can practice after," Eve said.

"Sound good."

"If you come to church with me tonight then you can sleep over." Eve sounded hopeful.

"That's still a no. But I'll see you tomorrow morning."

"Would you want to stay for dinner, too?"
"I can't... I have a date. I *think*."
"Really? With who?" Again, she had a big smile.
"Rodney. He said he'd pick me up at seven tomorrow night." Her smile disappeared. "Baron Rodney?"
"I guess. He is the co-captain of the football team."
"Yes, that's Baron." She seemed to have spaced out for a minute. But then she took a deep breath then said, "Leona, you seem the type of person who always wants to figure things out for herself. I won't say too much. Just be careful with him. He has a reputation of being somewhat... aggressive."

IN ART CLASS, I just got started on the Wax Vine drawing when someone sat next to me.

"Hi Leona."

I looked, wondering who she was. "Hi?"

"My name is Jenean Waters."

She looked familiar but I couldn't put my finger where I'd seen her.

"I play second-string sweeper. I came over to introduce myself. Being that you are co-captain and all."

I looked away from her, resting my gaze on my drawing. I didn't know how I felt about getting all this attention over the new position. "How long have you been playing?"

"I did their training camp over the summer... before my freshmen year. I was second-string sweeper last year, too. What about you? How long have you been playing?"

"I've been playing since middle school." I left it at that. "What's you place of origin?"

"USA," she said, sounding annoyed.

An idea popped into my head. "Hey Jenean, if I get the okay from Mr. Littmen, would you want to make a chess board with me?"

"Sure. Why not? What's your place?"

"Hawaii." She stood there, clearly thinking.

I went on. "Hawaii is a part of the United States, but they still have their own little world. They have a slightly different kind of culture. Chess is like a game of war. It could be like Hawaii is fighting the U.S. to stay different."

Jenean's face lit up. "That's a great idea."

I got the okay from Mr. Littman and smoothed over the details with Jenean.

IT'S LATE. All I wanted to do was go home. At my locker with Eve, I spotted someone walking straight for us. "Eve, who is that girl heading this way?"

She turned around. "That's Bridget Little. She's the captain of the team."

I finish collecting my things. Next thing I know, Bridget was standing next to me.

"Eve, will you excuse yourself so we can talk in private?"

Oh, man this girl was rubbing me the wrong way already. With a clear tone of attitude, I said, "Actually I was talking with her. You can wait."

One of Bridget's eyebrows arched. Eve quickly jumped in. "Its okay, Leona. Call me when you get home."

I nodded and she left. I turned to Bridget. "Yes?"

"I just wanted to offer you an opportunity to hang out with Genevieve and me tomorrow. We'll be at the docks from about one."

An opportunity? "Thank you, but I have plans."

"Leona. Hanging out with Bible-thumpers isn't the best thing for your image. Now that you're a captain, you need to start thinking about things."

Finding It

"Hanging out with you would better my image?" I was completely annoyed.

She tilted her head as if to say, "naturally."

"Coming from a girl who has been first string for..." I pretended to be thinking. I gasped. "A whole day." I took a step toward her and calmly said, "I managed to become a starter and co-captain without an image. I think I'll do just fine without you."

"Fine. Suit yourself." She whipped her hair around as she walked away.

I didn't know people like her actually existed.

Out in the parking lot, Leland and Maka were waiting for us, shirtless again.

"You know," I glanced at each of them. "There's this amazing invention. It helps keep you warm on chilly days like this. It's fairly new to our generation. It's called a *shirt*. Have you ever heard of it?"

Leland and Maka looked at each other, then back at me. "Nope."

I rolled my eyes.

"How did you do on the ASPHAP today?" Eve asked.

"I did well. More than half the jobs are available to me."

"Have you chosen one yet?" I asked Lee.

"Nope."

"Is it your mom or dad that wouldn't approve of you joining?" Eve asked.

"Mom." Lee and I spoke at the same time.

When we got home, Mom congratulated me. I turned to go to my room, but then I remembered. "Hey Mom, am I allowed to date?"

She looked at me with a smile. "Yes, you're allowed to date."

"Great, because I have a date tomorrow night at seven." I did my best to make it sound like it's not a big deal.

"What?" Leland snapped.

"Ooooohhhh." Mom perked up. "What's his name? When can I meet him?"

"Mom, please don't."

"I'm just asking a few questions," she said, innocently.

"His name is Rodney and you can meet him tomorrow." I left quickly.

When I grabbed my phone, I noticed that Rodney had already texted me.

"What's ur address? I can't pick you up unless I know where u live."

I texted him back: *"Mom wants to meet you before I leave."*

His response was faster than I expected. *"Sure ill meet the folks. What u thought I would just honk the horn n let u come 2 me."*

Then I texted Greg. *"Hey you free to Skype Sunday morning?"* This was the first time that I actually had a weekend free. Shoot, this was the first time I had anything planned for any weekend.

"Sure I work until 11pm night before. I'll Skype you at 11am."

I say *okay* and laid down, thinking about my plans. Life finally seemed to be looking up. For once, I was actually excited for the weekend.

7

Mom was in the kitchen cooking breakfast. Right away, I know something was up. "Good morning, Mom."

"Good morning, sweetheart."

"What's up? You never cook breakfast on the weekends."

"Nothing is going on. I just figured you and I could have a girls' morning, that's all."

She wanted to ask about Rodney.

"Where are Dad and Leland?"

"Your father is working. Leland is with someone named Maka. I've never heard of such a name."

"That's Eve's brother. Which by the way do, can you give me a ride to Eve's for practice? I'll text Leland for the ride home."

"Aren't you going on your date tonight?" She set a plate of food and a cup of apple juice in front of me.

I braced myself for the conversation. "I'll be back in plenty of time."

"What time is he going to be here?" She sat across from me with her breakfast.

"He said he'd be here by seven."

Mom smiled. "So, did you meet him at school?"

I began to eat.

"Actually, I first met him the night Leland and I went to the pizza diner."

"What grade is he in?"

"Mom, how many questions?"

"I'm just asking the basics. Your father and I will talk to him together, when we meet him tonight."

"Dad is going to be here?" He hadn't been home before eight since we'd moved here.

"Yes. I told him about your date and he promised he would be home in time to meet the boy."

No doubt a promise coerced by my mother. "He's a senior. Before you ask, I honestly don't know too much about him. He's the co-captain of the football team."

"Co-captain and his name is Rodney."

It was silent as we finished eating. Just when I thought I was in the clear, Mom said, "Leona. A first date is very exciting. But above all, I want you to remember something. There is no rule that says you have to finish the date with a kiss."

I rolled my eyes.

"Do you need help picking out something to wear?"

"Can't I just wear jeans and a shirt? We are only going to dinner and a movie."

"Jeans, yes. But you have to be selective about the shirt you wear. The shirt alone can make your outfit formal, semi-formal, or casual. Can I help you pick one out?"

Just to humor her, I said, "Yes. But I'm not picking it out until I get back from Eve's. Okay?"

I started collecting the dishes to wash them. Mom settled next to me to dry. "I'm going to ask you a question and you don't have to answer me if you don't want to." I nodded, wondering what kind of question she could possibly thought of.

"Have you ever tried... *you know*."

Finding It

I put down the dish that I was washing. I looked my mom square in the eye and finished her sentence. "You mean *have sex?*"

She smiled bashfully and nodded.

"No." I returned to the dishes. "I think sex should be a bigger deal then what people make it out to be. I have only ever seen drama erupt between two people because of it."

"What do you mean?"

"I saw this girl, at Starborough, go crazy on this guy because they had sex. To her, it meant something. To him… he said it was just friendly fun." I paused for a moment. "I think there is more involved with sex then just physical pleasure. I would rather die never having done it than deal with that kind of drama," I said honestly.

We continued to talk, surprisingly, about everything. I did warn her about what happened with Ms. Colner. She said that she was disappointed, but that she couldn't say she was surprised. When it came time to drive me to Eve's, we pretty much had run out of things to talk about. As mad as I was at her a few days ago, today I was noticing a different side of her. I don't know that we'd make it a habit, but it was nice talking to her.

Before I got out of the car, I let Mom know that Leland said we would be home around four. I closed the door and when I turned around, Eve was waiting for me at the door.

"Hi, Leona. How are you?"

"Good, you?" I asked, approaching the door.

"Good. Come on in. I hope you don't mind, but I invited a few people."

When I stepped inside, Mrs. Aquino was there to give me a hug and a kiss on the cheek. "It's good to see you again."

"It's good to see you, too."

We went into the dining room. There was a redhead already sitting at the table with another girl. They looked just alike.

"You remember Susan Thatcher from school? That's Beverly, her younger sister," Eve said.

We waved at each other awkwardly.

"We're still waiting on Jenean." Eve took a seat next to me.

When Jenean arrived, we ate and practiced. Spoke about Bridget and her two friends, Genevieve and Kayla. Apparently, there was major friction between this group and them.

While we were practicing, Leland and Maka showed up in the backyard. I figured this was a good time to wrap up. We played until Beverly made another goal and then said goodbye. Leland and I were the first to leave.

Lee and I were quiet until we were almost home.

"What time is this *date* of yours?"

I looked at him. He didn't sound happy with the idea.

"At seven, why?"

He inhaled deeply. "I asked Maka about him."

"Really, Leland?" I blurted out the words. "Do you really have nothing better to do then to check up on my date?"

He parked the car. "Just shut up a minute, will ya?"

I crossed my arms over my chest, raised my eyebrows, and waited for him.

"Maka said that he has only been at Moywood since his sophomore year. When he moved, here the word was that he had forced a female classmate to *be with him*. That his family moved here to get away from the gossip."

I didn't know what to think. "So, does anyone know if the accusations were true?"

He looked away. "I don't know. I don't think so."

"Then I'll bring mace," I said, jokingly. He didn't laugh. "And I won't go anywhere private. Dinner, movie, home. That's it."

"Promise?"

"I promise on one condition. Don't tell Mom and Dad what you heard. No sense in worrying them about something when we don't even know if it's true."

He contemplated this for a moment. "Okay."

One step in the door and Mom ran into the living room. "Leona, go take a shower. Now."

I turned to Leland. "Was she like this for your first date?"

He shook his head and whispered, "Mom didn't know about my first date."

I turned to her. "I'm going to take a shower but I am not going to start getting ready until six o'clock." I walked away before she had a chance to reply.

After my shower, I went ahead and finished the history paper I'd neglected in the computer lab. I was reading it through and editing it when my mother came barging in.

"So, I think I've narrowed the choices down to two shirts."

I looked at the clock. It was two minutes past six. Mom already had her hands in my closet. She pulled out two shirts. Both were satin, one yellow with a fairly low square neckline, short-sleeved. The second was an aqua, sleeveless shirt that would cover the whole chest area. And it had ruffles down the center. I picked the aqua shirt. "I think these jeans would go best with that shirt."

"Skinny jeans, Mom? Just what kind of shoes would I wear?"

"My heels."

I stared at her long enough for her to get the clue that my answer was *no*. She put them back and I pulled out a pair of black jeans and some black sneakers. She looked at me with disapproval. "Mom, I said you could help pick out the *shirt*."

"Fine, fine. Come on." She grabbed me by my hand and pulled me to her bathroom.

I groaned when I saw her makeup bag. Knowing I couldn't fight this, I said, "Mom, don't cake it on."

"I won't, I promise." She smiled. "I'm only going to put on some eyeliner, eye shadow, and mascara. Maybe some clear gloss, as well."

As she was applying the eye shadow, my father walked in.

"Since when do you wear makeup?" He saw my expression and nodded. "Lillian, why are you putting that stuff on her? The boy asked her for a date without it. I don't think it would matter much whether she wears any tonight."

"Lucas, go change and wait in the living room." She didn't even look away.

He gave me a sympathetic look.

"You see, Leona, with just the right amount of makeup you can complement your natural features. You should show off your beautiful brown eyes." She handed me gloss. "Here, take my little black purse. Bring the gloss, your wallet. and your cell phone. I'll get your debit card... just in case."

I put the gloss in the purse and headed to my room. When I got there, Leland was sitting in my computer chair. I gasped, almost having a heart attack. "Jeeezz, Lee. What are you doing in here?"

"Close the door."

I closed the door.

"Is that the purse you're taking?"

I nodded.

He stood up and took a few steps toward me. "I know you don't have mace. But I want you to take this." He showed me a black and red pocketknife. "Just press this button and the blade comes out on this side."

"Seriously? No. Lee, I'm not taking that." I tried to push it away.

He snatched the purse, shoving the knife inside. "Just take it. Give it back at the end of the night if you don't want to keep it."

I don't like guns. I don't like knives. I don't like the idea of having either one of them, ever. I most likely won't ever use it. "Do you really think this is necessary?"

He shrugged. "I don't know. I don't want to chance it, either. My going to the military would disappear if anything happened to you. I want you to be able to protect yourself.

I nodded apprehensively.

"Now get ready before Mom has a spaz attack." He left, closing the door behind him.

By the time I finished my hair, it was ten minutes to seven.

Finding It

When I heard the doorbell, I started getting dressed. I only had my pants on when Mom knocked on the door.

"Come in."

"Sweetheart, he's here. He's so handsome."

I rolled my eyes. "Here's the bank card." She put it on the desk as I finished putting on my shirt. "You look beautiful." I looked at her and saw a kind of smile that I'd never seen before. I put on my sneakers and looked at Mom. That was when I realized she'd begun to cry.

"Mom."

She interrupted me. "I'm okay. I'm fine. Go, don't keep him waiting alone with your father and brother."

I gave my mother a kiss on the cheek, grabbed the card, my wallet, and phone. They went into the purse. I checked my hair one last time in the mirror and walked to the living room.

When I stepped into the room, Rodney stood up. He was wearing black jeans with a red-collared, buttoned-down long-sleeved shirt. "Good evening, Leona. You look beautiful."

"Thank you. You look great, too," I said, bashfully.

"Yeah, yeah, yeah, whatever. Sit down. We're not done talking," Leland said obnoxiously.

He stood with his arms crossed over his chest. Dad sat in his recliner, smiling at me.

I sat on the couch next to Rodney. There was barely enough room for another person to sit between us. But Leland somehow managed to squeeze in, forcing a seat between us.

"Okay, so we know what your grades look like. We know what sports you play throughout the year. What do you plan on doing after high school, son?" Dad didn't seem at all tense.

"I'm going to Southern Vermont College. I'm going for business administration and management with a minor in communication."

"That's sounds good. Why that field?"

"Well my family owns a handful of businesses. We have a few

restaurants, groceries stores, and department stores. I plan on helping my father continue his father's success."

My mother entered the room. She settled on the love seat by my father.

Dad continued asking questions. "Sounds like a solid plan. Is it your plan or does it belong to your parents?"

"Honestly, it was always my parents' plan for all their kids to play a part in the family business. Mine was always something along the lines of pro athlete or astronaut. But as I grew older, reality set in that either choice wasn't a good plan. Going into the family business isn't just a good choice, but it would be something I could be proud of. Especially since I would be the only one of their children to join the business."

I looked at Rodney as he spoke and he wasn't even breaking a sweat.

This would be a good time to make our exit. "Okay, we better get going."

Everyone but my father stood up immediately. After my mom said goodbye to Rodney and me, my father finally stood and said, "Baron, kids these days do what they please. Whether it's with the approval of their parents or not, you guys seem to find a way and a place to do whatever you want. So, I won't tell you not to. What I will say is, touch my daughter in a manner that she does not approve of and you'll have more to worry about than just jail. Do I make myself clear?"

"Yes, sir."

"Good." They shook hands. Just before we made it to the door, my father added, "She is to be back no later than eleven o'clock."

"Yes, sir."

I started pushing him through the door. We walked together to his truck. He opened the door for me. I looked back at my house and all three them were watching us through the living room window.

"Sorry about Leland and my dad." I didn't know what else to say.

"It's okay," he said. "I'd be a little worried if they didn't threaten me. I would do the same thing for my niece if I'm around for any of her dates."

"You have a niece? How old is she?"

"She is going to be three."

"What's her name?"

"Her name is Delilah."

"That's pretty."

We stuck to small talk until we got to the restaurant. He opened the doors for me. Even though there was a crowd of people waiting, when the hostess saw us, we were seated almost immediately. We ended up sitting in a corner booth that was far too large for just the two of us.

The waiter walked up. "What can I get for you tonight, Baron?"

Okay, so the staff knows him.

"I'll have a Coke, Stella, and she'll have..."

"I'll have a sweet tea, please."

"I'll get it to you right away." Stella briskly walked away.

"How does the staff know you? Do you work here?" I asked.

"Kind of. This is one of the restaurants my family owns. I work here on the weekends and during the week when someone calls off."

"Oh, then maybe you could suggest what's good to eat."

"Sure, do you like chicken, beef, seafood, or are you a vegetarian?"

"I like seafood."

"Then turn to the last two pages. Just expect everything you order to have a small kick to it. All the recipes are supposed to be from Louisiana. Personally, I always enjoy the crab legs. It comes with homestyle-cut potatoes sautéed with eggs and shrimp on the side."

"The side sounds a little weird, but I'll try it."

The waiter came with our drinks. "Do you know what you would like?"

"Yes, we will take two orders of the snow crab legs with the usual side, please."

"Okay... any appetizers for you tonight?"

Rodney looked at me so I answered. "No, I want to save my appetite for the crab."

"Got it, coming right up."

"I guess it's a good thing I wore a sleeveless shirt," I said, jokingly, as I tugged on his shirt.

He thought for a moment. "Would you be offended if I took off this shirt? I have an undershirt on underneath."

"No, I wouldn't be offended. But that isn't at all fair." He leaned on the table, looking at me as if puzzled. "If you get anything on your undershirt, that's fine, but I only have this one shirt. I don't think my dad would be too thrilled at the idea of me coming home to change my shirt. Who knows the thoughts that would run through his mind?" I teased.

He smiled, then pressed his lips together thoughtfully. "I have an idea. I'll be right back." He walked past the bar.

While he was gone, I couldn't help but wonder if Rodney was being cheap or if I should be honored that he brought me to his family's restaurant. I assumed that he wouldn't have to pay for the meal. I was sure word would get to his parents about the girl he'd brought to dinner.

Rodney returned with something black in his hand. "One for you and one for me." He handed me an apron. "They have a box full of them in the back."

I smiled at the bright idea. "That's fair." I busied myself with tying the apron. "Rodney tell me, did you ask me out because I got co-captain?" I looked up to see his reaction.

He sat up straighter, inhaled and exhaled. "In a way, yes." He sat back and rested his arm on the ledge of the booth. "When I saw you at the pizza diner, I thought you were beautiful. When you said you were confident, I thought you were cocky. So, when I heard you're a starter and got co-captain. I…" He trailed off as if he was thinking of the right thing to say. "It's impressive."

Just then, the food came. As strange as the side had sounded, it tasted great. We were about halfway through eating when Rodney chuckled.

With my mouth full of garlic bread, I asked, "What?"

"You surprise me is all."

I tried to think briefly of something I could have done or said. "I don't get it."

"Most girls on the first date get something like water and a salad. The last thing I expected you to eat is crab legs. I'm not saying it's a bad thing. It's a pleasant surprise."

"Unless the salad comes with a meal, I don't eat salad. If it's good, I have no problem eating something messy."

We drove to the theater with twenty minutes to spare. We played video games while we waited.

After the movie, I started over-thinking things and totally freaked out. *I wouldn't mind a kiss… but what do I do? What do I do with my hands? Am I supposed to go for the kiss, or is he? Wait, we haven't even held hands. Can we kiss before we've held hands?*

He pulled into my driveway. Like every other stop, he helped me out of his truck. We walked to the porch and sat on a bench. We began to talk about the movie, our families, and school.

"You keep talking and you'll be more than just ten minutes past curfew." My father said, looking directly at Rodney. "You're lucky her mother saw when you pulled in. Five minutes and I want her in the house." He went back inside before I could say anything.

"Well, I guess this means goodnight," Rodney said. We both stood and I was thinking, *Oh, my God, this is it*. He leaned over and laid a soft, tender kiss on my cheek.

"Good night, Leona."

"Good night, Rodney."

He turned and walked away. I went into the house.

"How did it go?" Mom asked.

I closed the door. "It went well."

"How well?" my father asked, suspiciously.

I stopped and looked him square in the eyes. "I will always be your baby." He smiled. I walked over to Leland's room. The door was open.

"Hey, how'd it go?"

I handed him the knife. "It went good."

"Keep it, I have another."

"I don't want it. Don't need it. Good night, Lee."

I got ready for bed. When I crawled into bed, I fell asleep with a smile. This time because I had a kiss on my cheek.

8

The dinner at the Aquino's house was uneventful. At least my dreams of going to Hawaii hadn't been squashed… yet.

In school, Spanish and English went by smoothly. I was at my locker when I noticed Rodney. My heart was pounding.

"Good morning." Rodney, again, leaned on the next locker.

"Good morning," I answered. I hoped he didn't notice how nervous I was.

"You didn't text me yesterday," he said.

I closed my locker door and leaned on it, facing him. "That goes both ways."

"This is true. Did you enjoy yourself Saturday night?"

"I did."

"I was hoping we could go out again Friday. I figured we could hang at the docks and then head to the CinéBistro after."

"The docks… isn't that where Bridget and Genevieve hang out?"

He nodded.

"I don't know."

"Come on. You'll be there for me, not for them." He flashed an amazing smile.

"Okay, then."

"Great. I'll pick you up at seven Friday night."

"Sounds good."

"What's your next class? I'll walk you."

"Art with Mr. Littman." We navigated the crowded corridor.

"Have you ever tried getting the perfect grade?"

"Not really. But there was this one kid who tried so hard to get it. He only handed in things for the challenge, so ended up failing art."

"Shut up. Seriously? What's his name?"

"Nicolai. That's him right there." He pointed out a short, skinny, pale-skinned blonde-haired boy. "Okay, text me sometime."

I walked into class and Jenean was already at a table with the board. We got right to work in silence.

I spent a few minutes wondering how to start a conversation with Nicolai. I finally just got up. "Nicolai, my name is Leona."

He looked at me with a smile. "What can I do for you?"

"I wanted to ask you about the art projects that you turned in for the challenge. I'm just trying to find something that would get a rise out Mr. Littman."

"Nothing gets a rise out of that man."

I kept pressing. "Maybe you could tell me what you did."

He sighed. "The only thing I think might help is that he doesn't seem too fond of paper. Things like drawings or paintings. For my Bermuda box, he looked disappointed. I got a smile out of him when I turned in my model of the Taj Mahal. On the board in the back, I painted a sunset and put lights in the roof to give it the illusion of the sun glistening. I turned it in December. Mr. Littmen said it was very impressive but it didn't make him say, 'Oh my God,' or 'Wow.' He ended up passing me the first half of the year because of that piece."

"Do you still have it?"

"The Taj?"

"Yeah."

"Yes. I saved everything I handed in."

Finding It

"Do you think we can arrange for me to see all your projects?"

He raised his eyebrows. "Seriously?"

I bit my bottom lip.

"I know I'm a stud muffin, but you don't have to beat around the bush. If you want to go on a date, all you have to do is ask."

I made an annoyed sound. "I'm not trying to be rude, but I have work to do. Are you going to help me, or not?"

"With all due respect, Leona." His attitude surpassed mine. "You don't know me and vice versa. Those projects are at my house. They are too big to bring in and quite frankly I don't care to invite you there. My answer is no." He turned back to face his clay. I went back to my seat, fuming.

When the bell rang, I asked Mr. Littmen if I could stay.

"Sure. I'll go get some lunch, you two continue working," Mr. Littmen said.

I turned and saw that Nicolai was still in the room. *Great.*

"What's your place of origin?" It was Nicolai.

"Hawaii. What's yours?"

"Argentina."

"That sounds hard."

He walked over and sat across from me, preparing to say something.

Mr. Littmen interrupted. "Mr. Coverdale, if you are going to be here, I expect you to be working."

He grabbed some paper and started drawing. "It's better than getting the Bermuda Triangle again. That's how I failed last year."

Mr. Littmen coughed loudly.

Nicolai rolled his eyes. "I mean, I failed because I didn't do the regular homework. But, having the Bermuda Triangle is one of the harder places."

Huh. "Mr. Littmen would you mind joining our conversation? I think I would benefit from your input."

"Sure."

I glanced over at Nicolai, who wore a smirk on his face.

Turning to Mr. Littmen, I asked, "What piece that Nicolai turned in impressed you most?"

"Are you okay with me discussing your work with another student?" Mr. Littmen asked Nicolai.

"Yeah, sure." He shrugged.

"All of his work was very good. But his most impressive work was his model of the Taj Mahal and the underwater box view of the Bermuda Triangle."

"Why didn't you give him the perfect grade?"

"Neither surprised me with that *wow* factor that I'm looking for."

I thought about it. "Mr. Littmen, why do you offer the challenge if the successes are so rare?"

"I see my students' full artistic potential and creativity through that challenge. With the art program always at risk of being cut, I want to see as much creativity as I can." He took a deep breath. "But the perfect grade shouldn't be as rare as you'd think. Sometimes a student will turn something in that is perfect grade worthy, but they hand it in to be graded. When that happens, naturally I give it an A."

"When was the last time that happened?" I asked.

"Three years ago. She was a freshman at the time. It was creative." Mr. Littmen looks beyond almost like he was imagining the project as he spoke. "It was well put together and well thought out. She handed me an index card with a single sentence that explained the whole thing."

"What did she do?" Curiosity consumed me.

"I can't discuss that without her permission."

"Who was it?" Nicolai asks. "Maybe we can ask her about it." I looked at Nicolai, not hiding my surprise.

Mr. Littmen seemed to be contemplating whether he should tell us or not when the bell rang. They both stood.

"Mr. Littmen, I would really like to know who she is."

His expression gave away nothing. "You know Miss Sentmore,

determination is not the only thing you need to get the perfect grade. I believe Mr. Coverdale can attest to that."

"Right now, sir, all I need is a name."

"Her name is Bridget Little." I cringed hearing the name. Nicolai looked at the floor, slowly shaking his head.

"Thank you, sir."

"Good luck."

I got an empty shoebox and piled in the pawns I'd managed to make. I wondered if Bridget still had that piece after three years. Maybe Rodney could borrow it. Halfway to my locker, I realized Nicolai was following me. I stopped short. "What are you doing?"

"Brainstorming with you. This is going to be hard, but I think we can pull it off," he said confidently.

"Since when did this become a duo?" My hand naturally landed on my hip.

"Since I can't enter myself, I might as well help someone who can," he said. "Besides, you ask way more questions than I ever did. If anyone can win it, I'm betting on you."

He seemed to genuinely want to help out. "Well, you can start helping by showing me your projects."

He tensed up a bit. "I don't know about that."

"Why not?"

"Life at my house..." He shrugged. "It sucks."

"Well, you think of a way for me to see your projects and I'll think of a way to see Bridget's. When, and I mean *when* I see your project, I'll share what I find out."

"Give me your number."

I did.

"I'm texting you my address. If, by early November, I don't show you my project, show up at my house."

"I'll do that."

"Great," he said. "So, for our first attempt, one of us should make friends with the beast. It should preferably be a beauty."

"You *are* talking about yourself, right?"

He rubbed his cheek and chin as if he was smoothing out a beard. "Why, thank you," he said with conceit.

I couldn't help but laugh at him.

"No, really, I was talking about you," Nikolai said.

I shook my head. "Can't be me. She tried to *make friends* with me last week and I blew her off. So, now I'm looking for a back-door approach. Like through a mutual friend or something."

"Who do you know that's mutual?"

"I have date with Baron Rodney. He's friends with her brother, Brad."

Nikolai scrunched up his face. "Okay, well you work that angle. I'll try and jimmy open the front door. I'll text you tonight," he said, walking away.

How did that just happen?

Eve and I were headed to practice when we met up with Susan and Jenean in the locker room. Out on the field, we waited on the bleachers for instructions. Bridget walked over with her friends. When she looked my way, she rolled her eyes. Yup, burned that bridge. They ended up sitting in the front.

"Okay, ladies." Coach Conner called out for our attention. "First, congratulations for making the team. If you don't know your positions, see Coach Ash after your run today. In case you don't know your captain, this year it's Bridget Little."

Bridget stood and slowly twirled as if she were modeling her gym clothes. I didn't bother to clap.

When she finally sat down, Coach continued. "And your co-captain is Leona Sentmore." I waved. "Keep in mind that positions can change at any time. Our first game is in two weeks against Simmons High School. Let's get to work. Ladies, go run your laps."

During practice, I could tell who favored Bridget over me. Every now and again I would suggest something to a teammate—the freshman and sophomores listened to me. But most of the juniors didn't. The seniors acted like I didn't exist. I heard Bridget suggesting the same thing I'd said, to the *same person* and they cooperated. It quickly grew frustrating.

When practice was over, we gathered on the bleachers for some announcements. Then to my surprise, Coach Conner said, "Coach Ash would like to speak to Eve and Kayla. Bridget and Leona, come see me. The rest of you ladies, we will see you tomorrow."

By the time I got to the bottom of the bleachers, Bridget was already talking to Conner. Coach held up her index finger, indicating for me to wait. I sat on the first row of the bleachers and looked over at Eve, who was with Kayla and Coach Ash. Kayla didn't seem to be pleased with the conversation. Coach Conner came toward me. Behind the coach, Bridget stomped off the field, clearly unhappy. Kayla and Eve were trailing behind her.

The two coaches sat next to me. "Okay, Leona," Conner said. "Coach Ash and I noticed you and Bridget don't seem to get along very well. What's going on?"

I told them about what happened on Friday, then about her little pride party - I didn't hold back.

"We've gotten a few complaints about her attitude from players. Hopefully, after today that'll cool down," Conner said.

"What am I supposed to do as co-captain, anyways?"

Conner explained what I already knew. She emphasized that I was to help everyone play as a team. "Are you sure I'm the right person for the job?" I asked.

"Coach Ash seems to think so."

Ash explained in a whisper hardly audible, "You are meant to be a leader."

"If you need to sign, I'm fluent in ASL."

She looked at me then began to sign. "When you saw that Eve was at risk of getting cut from the team, I overheard you making plans to practice with her. She came back the next day with a new determination. We don't know what you did but whatever it was, it worked." Ash continued, "I understand that you've been practicing with some of the other players as well." I nodded to confirm. "We need that kind of leadership on this team."

"Not everyone cares to listen to me," I pointed out.

"We'll figure out a fix for that," Conner responded. "See you tomorrow."

In the locker room, everyone was gone except for Eve.

"What did Ash say to you?" I asked.

"She just explained why they didn't have a first and second-string goalie." Eve said. "I'll be goalie for the first half and Kayla will play the second half. I overheard Bridget saying that people complained about her attitude. What did they talk to you about?"

"Nothing much," I said casually. "They noticed some of the players wouldn't listen to me and asked me about it. Are you ready to go?"

"Ready... any word on the Hawaii trip yet?" Eve asked.

"No. But your mom and my mom seemed to get along really well."

"Hey, I almost forgot," Eve said abruptly. "The girls are coming over to practice again this Saturday. You are obviously invited. But I could use you help later that night... for babysitting."

"Uh-oh." Leland, waiting in the parking lot overheard the last part. "Babies don't like Leona."

I shoved him. "Babies have always made me nervous. It's a fragile life in my hands, something I try to avoid. How old are the kids?"

"It will be *six kids*. Two are under a year old. The others are between five and nine. It would be for no more than three hours and we would each get sixty bucks."

"Okay. You take the babies. I can handle the kids."

"Deal."

We went our separate ways. When we got home, I opened the door and froze at the entryway. Dad sat in his recliner and mom stood with her hands on her hips. Clearly, one of us was in trouble. Leland peered over my shoulder to see why I'd stopped.

I could practically feel his breath on my neck as he casually asked, "What's up?"

"Leona, will you please give us some privacy? Your father and I have something to discuss with your brother." My mother's tone wasn't friendly.

I walked past them, into the hallway and stopped just around the corner.

"I got an interesting call from your school today," Mom said.

"Okaaay," Leland said.

"They said you weren't in school until after lunch on Friday. Care to explain?"

I slapped myself on the forehead, having completely forgotten that the school calls home for absences. I snuck a glance around the corner. Both my parents had their backs to me. Leland had his fingers intertwined behind his neck and his gaze focused on the ceiling. He flopped onto the couch. I hid back around the corner.

"Son," my dad said calmly, "Your mom is thinking the worst. I happen to believe there is a reasonable explanation. But you need to clue us in."

After a moment of silence, I heard someone sigh.

"I spent most of the morning taking the ASPHAP test."

Wow. To my surprise, Leland had answered truthfully.

"What is that?" Mom asked.

Dad cleared his throat... it was an unmistakable sound we'd heard all of our lives. "It's a test someone would take to see what jobs they would eligible for... in the military."

Mom gasped. "No!" She began to cry. "No... you... you said you were thinking about medical school just... last week."

"I lied," Leland said. His voice held no remorse. "I don't want to go to college. I want to work, travel. I want a *career*."

"You could get all of that in college," Mom said, her voice still shaky.

I had to look around the corner again. Dad still sat in his chair. His elbow on the arm of the chair, he had his hand balled up, resting his chin on his fist. Mom must have sat down on the love seat. Leland was on the couch with his elbow on his knees and his face in his hands.

"No, Mom... you can't." He looked up and caught me peeking around the corner. "Not the same way that you can in the military. Do you know how many people graduate and don't end up working in the field of their degree?"

"What about architecture? For the longest time you've loved to build things." Mom was pleading.

"Only two percent of people that study that field make it successfully." Leland argued with facts.

"I won't let you do it. I won't let you join," Mom stated.

"Mom, I love you." His tone was low and gentle. "But I don't need your approval. Come January first, I turn eighteen, I can sign the paperwork for myself."

I hear my mom walking toward me, so I ran to my room. When I heard her bedroom door close, I came back out.

"Dad, will you just say something?" Leland pleaded.

"Are you sure this is what you want to do?"

"Yes."

"Then I am happy for you, son. It sounds like you did your research. I hope it's everything you want and nothing you don't." I heard patting, which I assumed was a male-bonding bear hug. "Have you chosen a job yet?" Dad asked.

"No, I haven't, but there are more than half the jobs available to me." After a short pause, Leland spoke again. "You think Mom is going to be okay with this?"

"She doesn't have a choice but to adjust. She'll be alright," Dad said. "What branch have you joined?"

Now that the drama was over, I went to my room and saw texts from Nicolai and Rodney. Nicolai said that he didn't have any luck with Bridget. After finishing homework and getting ready for bed, I called Rodney and spoke with him until Dad told me it was time wrap it up.

9

I was in bliss. I saw Rodney. I managed to get through the conversation without blushing. I spoke with Nicolai, who said that he was going to have to talk to Bridget again—away from her friends. Apparently, her attitude was worse when her posse was around as an audience.

∼

AT PRACTICE, Eve and I walked out to the field to see Coach Conner separating the players into two groups.

"Leona, you're on this team," Conner instructed. "Eve, you are on that team."

I looked at my team and, with the exception of Bridget, I had all seniors and a few juniors on my team. Not one freshman or sophomore. Coach handed everyone on my team a neon green belt. We began to scrimmage. Periodically, the coaches would switch some of the players around.

By the end of the third game, tension on both teams was running high. My team made a goal and I saw Genevieve yelling at Susan and pointing at the goal. From the little I heard, Genevieve was blaming Susan for the last goal. I ran over and squeezed between them. As Susan backed away, Genevieve moved forward.

"Susan, just walk away. I'll keep Gen off you."

Susan slowly walked off, her head hung low. I pushed Genevieve with enough force to get her to take a step back. "Cut it out, Gen. It's only *practice*."

"If she can't play right now, then she shouldn't be on this team," she yelled.

"Well, with your poor sportsmanship, maybe you shouldn't be on it, either."

"Back off." Bridget jammed herself between the two of us. She put her hands on Gen's shoulders and asked if she was okay. When she nodded, they both turned and walked away.

I look around and everyone was watching, including the coaches. From across the field, using ASL, I signed: "Why didn't you do anything?"

Coach shrugged. "We wanted to see what would happen."

"Then I won't get in trouble for pushing her?"

"No," she signed. "Just don't do it again."

Slightly frustrated, I responded, "Fine."

After the last scrimmage, Conner told everyone they were dismissed, but started calling individuals to the bleachers. Just when I thought I was in the clear, she called me as well. I sat with Eve, Jenean, and Susan. Bridget, Kayla, and Genevieve sat the row below us.

"This division on the team begins here with you seven," Conner said. "When your captain asks you to do something, don't ignore her. Genevieve, that goal you yelled at Susan for, got through ten other people besides Susan. I don't know how this started. And I honestly don't care. You need to be able to have mutual respect for each other on the field. You have to be able to work together."

Coach Ash tapped Conner's shoulder and nodded at me to interpret. "We can't expect to win anything with a broken or divided foundation."

"We aren't looking to reprimand any of you, but if this doesn't clear up, then we will. Am I understood?" Conner asked

Murmurs were heard. "Yes ma'am." Some girls just nodded.

We were dismissed and, after meeting Leland to go home, I headed straight to my room to get started on my homework.

I had two assignments left when I heard my father calling me to the kitchen. Mom hadn't said much since she found out about Lee's plans for the military. Slightly annoyed, I went to the kitchen only to find both my parents and Mrs. Aquino sitting there, waiting for me.

"What's up?" I asked.

"Well honey," Mom said. "As you know, your father and I have been discussing this trip to Hawaii."

I held my breath.

"We have never said *no* to anything you have asked. Usually, it would be against our better judgment to let you go. But since Moana doesn't seem the type to sell your organs on the black market, we've decided to let you go."

"Yes!" I screamed, shooting my hands in the air.

They sat back, laughing at my reaction.

"However," Dad said. "There will be some rules you have to follow."

I sat down and listened attentively. "We will be writing a check from your account to Moana for the airline ticket."

"Okay." I was so excited, I could barely sit still.

"When time gets closer, we are going to put three-hundred dollars of your money onto a prepaid MasterCard for souvenirs, food, clothes, or whatever."

"Question."

"What?"

"If I make any money like babysitting or something, can I give you that money to add to the prepaid card?"

My dad looked at my mom and nodded once. My mother smiled.

"Yes," he said. "We won't give you that card until we take you to the airport. Now, you must keep up your grades. No more tussles with anyone—especially your teachers. If you break any rules of any kind, you won't be going. Am I understood?"

"Yes, sir." I said. "Have you told Eve yet?" I asked Moana.

"No, I have not."

"I have got to tell her." I started running for my room, but skidded short of the doorway. I turned around. "Are we done talking?"

All three laughed. "Yes, Leona, we are," Dad answered.

I took off running. I barged into Leland's room and told him I got the okay to go to Hawaii. I darted out before he had a chance to say anything. On my phone, I saw a text message from Rodney. Before responding, I texted Eve that Hawaii was a go.

She responded with, "Yay! I can't wait. It's going to be so much fun! I planned some special things for us to do."

When I sat down at my desk, I read the text from Rodney. "Hey beautiful." I blushed. I've never had anyone call me *beautiful* before. I didn't really know how to respond, so I went for a sure thing. "Hey."

He answered in less than ten seconds. "Took you a bit to respond is everything okay?"

Excitement built up in me all over again. "Yes. I was just talking with my parents about a trip to Hawaii that I am going on with Eve."

"Oh man can I go with you?"

"No. I think you would be a distraction. I am going with a mission in mind."

"Which would be?"

I wonder if he really cared. "Finding something that would inspire a perfect grade in art class."

"Good luck. Many have tried, many have failed."

"I won't."

Finding It

"You know your confidence is becoming a very attractive feature."

"Thank you. Hey, I don't mean to cut you off but I still have homework to finish."

"Say no more. Try not to think about me. I'll see you tomorrow."

I finally start working on my homework again. A thought popped into my mind. All my life in Camden, I'd not had one friend. It seemed like I've made two friends in less than two weeks. I never even had a candidate for a boyfriend and now I'd been on a first date with plans for another. I don't know what people here see that people in Camden hadn't. It's frustrating to think of how, for fifteen years, I was a source for people's humor. I didn't think I'd changed.

But it would have been nice to have known someone like Eve, who'd ask me if something was wrong. Or someone like Rodney who said that I was pretty. Or someone like Nicolai or Jenean who had indirectly said that I was worth working with.

How was it that Coach Ash could see leadership potential and no one else ever did? Maybe the people here in Woodstock were just deluding themselves. Maybe I was just worth less than what they thought.

I managed to finish my homework, then took a shower and got into bed. Comparing my life changes became overwhelming. So, I switched to stressing out about what I should pack for the trip. What were the chances of my parents letting me go? But, hey, they *were* letting me go, so no complaints from me.

10

After getting ready for school, I went into the kitchen and noticed Mom standing by a window with a cup of coffee, just watching the rain. I got that she wasn't thrilled by Leland joining the military, but enough was enough. I sat down and ate silently.

When I finished, I said, "Good morning, Mother."

"Good morning." Her voice wasn't anywhere close to cheerful.

"Would Lee joining the military be that bad for him?"

"If the worst should happen... I don't know what I would do..." Her words trailed off.

Every word that came out of her mouth made me more infuriated. This wasn't about her concern for Leland. This was about *her*.

"God, Mom, this isn't about you! It's about *Leland*."

She stood by the window like a statue.

I huffed. "It's about him having a dependable source of income plus benefits. He doesn't want to be stuck at home writing a book... just hoping someone will buy it."

"Lee!" Leland was at the front door. He jerked his head. Time to go. I glanced back at Mom, who still hadn't moved. I rolled my eyes and left.

The drive to school was silent.

"Hey, Leona."

I turned. "Hey Nick, what's up?"

"Nothing. I haven't heard from you in a few days. I wanted to see where we were with the whole *Bridget project* thing."

Just then the bell rang and I lost my train of thought. I shook my head as if to clear my mind. "I'll try and talk to Bridget and I'll text you tonight."

"Okay, take it easy."

In Spanish class, my phone vibrated. I waited for Mr. Sanchez to finish talking. When I looked at my phone, it was a text message from my father saying, "Call me now." I immediately felt tension. Besides the fact that he wanted me to call him during school hours, there was the fact that my dad never texted. This meant I was in trouble.

I excuse myself to the bathroom and called.

"Hello?"

"Hey Dad, what's going on?"

"What happened this morning with your mother?"

Chances were he already knew, so I relayed everything truthfully.

"From what I heard, your reaction was just as bad, if not worse than what you think of your mother's." Although he wasn't yelling, his tone sounded angry. "When you get home tonight, you are going out with your mother. You are going to talk to her and you are going to apologize for the way you spoke to her."

"I can't, Dad. I have a date with Rodney tonight."

"Cancel it," he demanded. "Because you are *not* going."

I knew better than to argue. "Yes, sir." He hung up without saying anything else. On my way back to class, I text Rodney to meet me at my locker after this period.

Rodney was already at my locker. "What's up?"

I sighed. "I have to cancel tonight."

"How come?"

"I got into some trouble this morning. I yelled at my mom and my dad told me to make it up to her... *tonight*."

He pressed his lips together pensively. "That's too bad... but are we still on for Sunday?"

"As far as I know, yes."

"I'll pick you up at noon, okay?"

I smiled.

"Okay. Behave until then."

I nodded bashfully, then asked him about talking to Brad, about Bridget's project. He said he would see what he could do. As he walked away, I noticed Bridget by herself.

"Bridget," I called.

When she saw it was me, her face went cold. "What?"

"Look, I get we don't like each other but I was hoping we could start over."

"I don't care to be friends with you," she blurted.

"I'm not saying that we have to be friends, I'm just saying maybe start fresh. Put the history behind us."

She crossed her arms. "I. Don't. Like. You."

"Fine." I just walked away.

In art, I set up the chess board with Jenean. We'd decorated the border with palm trees and sand. Nicolai watched. Mr. Littmen looked it over. Finally, he took a seat in a nearby chair.

"Every fifteenth of December and, again in May, we hold an art show to help raise money for the school," he said. "I only display the artwork that gets an A-grade. I would like to display this. But I'd need your approval."

"So... you are giving it an A?" I asked.

He nodded. "As long as we get an A, who cares where you display it?" Jenean said.

"Sounds good." I shrugged.

Mr. Littmen moved away.

"Did you watch him?" Nick said. "If he was impressed, you

couldn't tell." He was right. Mr. Littmen had a better poker face then my father.

When class was over, Nick walked with me to my locker. "Did you talk to Bridget?" He asked, leaning against a locker.

"Yes, but I got nowhere. She is a green-nosed witch."

"With a wart on it," he added jokingly. "There has to be some way to see it."

"Well… I spoke with Rodney. He said he'd talk to Brad to see if she still has it."

"Wait a minute." He exclaimed standing up straight. "Mr. Littman said he gave it an A."

"Okaaaay?" I said, wondering where he was going with this.

"He just said that anything that gets an A gets displayed in the art show." He rummaged in his backpack. "Students from the school newspaper and yearbook club take pictures at events like that. Those pictures are archived *somewhere*." He pulled out his phone and sent a text.

"Who are you texting?"

"My friend Charley. He works for the school newspaper and the yearbook. He says the photographers have the cameras attached to their eyes."

"Cool. Do you think he'd talk with us today?"

"That's what I am trying to find out. I'll text you," he said, walking away.

WHEN I GOT HOME. I put my bags in my room and went to my mother's room. "Mom, if you wouldn't mind, I'd like to treat you to dinner and ice cream." I did my best to sound upbeat.

"Your dad mentioned something about it. I'll start getting ready." She still sounded gloomy.

We left and went to an ice cream parlor called *Dale's*. I'd seen it the night Leland and I went for pizza. Mom and I ordered chicken wraps. By the time we'd finished eating, there were only about six other people in the shop. I honestly couldn't think of what to say to her. So, I just apologized. "Mom, I'm sorry for this morning. I was out of line. I didn't mean to hurt you."

"It's okay, honey. I told you what I was thinking about this morning. But there's something that bothers me more than that."

I looked at my mother. Even though she wasn't looking my way, I knew her eyes had begun to water.

"I'm listening, Mom," I said gently.

She took a moment to regain her bearings. "Your grandfather passed away when you were seven, so you don't remember too much about him. He retired after twenty-eight years in the Army. He was fun, but still very strict. We had to finish homework before playing. Manners always had to be correct – especially at the table." She took a sip of her milkshake. "I remember I woke up once in the middle of the night when I was nine. I went to the kitchen for a glass of water. Once in the kitchen, I saw my father's hand swinging. He struck my mother. I'd always noticed bruises on her, but that was the first time I realized how she'd gotten them. He never hit me for some reason... it was always her. Years later, when my mother got sick, I asked her why she stayed with him. Her answer was, 'He was never like that before the military. I hoped to, once more, see the man I fell in love.' The last thing I expected to see was my mother smile in the hospital bed. But a smile did come across her face and she said, 'I'm glad I did stay, because he eventually did come back to me. The Liam I married is back.'

My mother sighed and forced a smile. "I didn't understand what she meant until my father came to the hospital later that night. He brought her a candlelight dinner, a teddy bear, and a bouquet her favorite flowers. I saw affection and romance. Something I'd never seen him show my mother before."

"I'm sorry, Mom. I didn't know." I really did feel bad now.

"I know, honey. I know. The thing is the military changes people. Some people change for the good. Some... not so good.

Logan was always the one to display a good sense of acumen. He was always level-headed. Leland is always going to be the one I see as lively and witty. The words I use to describe him may change after he joins. Selfishly, I don't know if I'm ready for that. Unselfishly," she sighed, "I don't know if he's ready for that."

She'd worried about the same thing that I had and I yelled at her for it. I could kick myself right about now.

Trying to lighten the mood, I asked, "What's the word you use to describe me?"

Without any hesitation, she said, "Decisive." A surge of pride went through my body. Then my mom chuckled and said, "Sometimes you're just downright pigheaded."

I couldn't help but laugh along with her. We continued to talk, then walked around and window-shopped. When we finally got home, it was nearly ten. Dad was in his recliner. He looked at me and raised his eyebrows. I nodded, confirming that I'd apologized.

I laid down, thinking about my mother. I wonder if there was more to that story. I fell asleep, thankful that my father was not like hers.

11

"Leona, sweetheart." Mom sat on my bed, shaking my shoulder. "Moana called me this morning. She said she could use my help making lunch today. We need to be at their house by ten, okay?"

I nodded sleepily, then start getting ready for the next twenty-four hours with Eve.

What happened last year was last year. Now, I had friends. Eve seemed like a heartfelt person. Nicolai seemed like a good guy. And Rodney, a very attractive football player, was interested in me.

At Eve's house, we were greeted and our moms got to work in the kitchen. "Who's coming this week? The usual?" I asked.

"No, Jenean is grounded. Susan and Beverly will be here," Eve answered.

"How long before lunch?"

"About an hour. Maka and his friends will be here, too."

She and I set the table. When we finished, Susan and Beverly showed up. The guys took up the two love seats, so we took the couch.

We were catching up when one of the guys interrupted us. "Eve, aren't you going to introduce me to your lady friends?" He spoke with an accent. He had short, black hair, bushy eyebrows and pale skin.

"Ladies," Eve waved an arm dramatically. "This... is *Domiano*."

He flashed us a two-fingered peace sign. Eve continued in a normal tone, pointing to the person next to him. "That is Donivan, that is Mark, sitting in the rocking chair."

Mark sat with us at lunch.

"Susan and Beverly, that's Leland sitting next to Maka. He's Leona's brother."

"You're Leona Sentmore?" Domiano asked.

"That's me."

He smiled. "You were quite the hot topic at the docks last night."

This guy sounded like a sleaze ball. I didn't like him.

But before I could say anything, Leland asked, "Why?"

"Bridget says Gen has the hots for Rodney. She said that Gen was ready to fight you on the field after you pushed her." He never once looked at Leland. He just kept looking at me like he was trying to get a rise out of me. "I hope I'm there to see *that* fight."

"Sorry to disappoint you, but there won't be any fight," I said.

"Are you sure? I think it would be a good one."

"Dom, don't be an instigator," Maka said.

"Come, it's time to eat."

Saved by Mrs. Aquino!

We prayed, we ate, and kept our conversations neutral. When we finished, the girls and I left to start practice. Unfortunately, the guys stuck around to watch.

Eve and I put on the goalie gear.

"When do I get to see you play, Leona?" Domiano hollered.

"If you don't leave my sister alone, I'm going to give you the fight you're looking for, Domiano." Leland sounded angry.

Eve hadn't noticed the tension. She'd been putting on her helmet. "I hope I do well."

"You'll do great. Which one of the guys are you trying to

impress?" I asked jokingly. Her face turned red and I realized she really was trying to impress one of them. Panicking, I asked, "It's not Damiano, is it?"

"Oh, for heaven's sake, no!" she whispered.

"We'll talk about it later. Show whoever it is why you're first string goalie."

"There is no first string, Leona."

"He doesn't know that." I winked. I moved up to sweeper and moved Beverly forward. Pretty soon, the guys left and, by the time Maka came back, Mom, Susan, and Beverly were gone. Mrs. Aquino, Maka, and I stood in the living room talking while Eve showered.

Maka was talking about the tournament with his mother.

"Is Leland going? He hasn't mentioned anything about it."

"If he goes, he can only watch. In our gym, you can't compete until you've trained there for six months," Maka answered.

"How long have you been training?" I asked him.

"I started in Hawaii when I was nine, with Judo."

"Makaio was always running around," said Mrs. Aquino. "We could never keep him still until my husband found Judo. They did it together and would come home exhausted. A mother's dream." She winked. "How did your chess board do? Have you handed it in yet?"

"Yes, we got an A. Mr. Littmen said he was going to display it at the art show, December fifteenth."

"Good, I'll be there."

"I have a few more ideas, but nothing worthy of a perfect grade. When we get to Hawaii, I'll have to find something absolutely breathtaking."

"I'm sure Kai will have plenty of places planned for you to see," Mrs. Aquino said.

"I'll show you the falls," Maka said.

Eve came in. "I'll make a list of things you'll need to pack."

"Good." I make sure to sound relieved. They all laughed at me.

Finding It

"What time am I picking you two up tonight?" Maka asked.

"Nancy said she'd be home no later than eleven-thirty," Eve answered.

"Okay, I'll show up at eleven, just in case."

I took a shower, then Eve and I worked on homework. When we finished, we had about forty-five minutes left.

I asked, "So which one is it?"

She smiled and her face turned bright red. "I knew you would ask. It's Donivan." I think back to when she had introduced all the guys. "The one that was sitting next to Damiano."

"Ooooohhh," I said, teasingly. "Where did you meet him?"

"We originally met at the gym last year. It wasn't until a few months ago that he started going to our church."

"Does he know you like him?"

She shrugged. "We exchanged numbers... we talk, but we haven't been on a date or anything."

"Why don't you just talk to him when you see him at the gym?"

"I always imagined that God would have me meet someone in the church."

"You seem pretty sure about this God thing," I said, slightly annoyed.

"I am."

"How?"

"Nothing makes sense without Him. You know how you learn in school because a book that was written years ago, then revised when new theories come out? But I believe in something that has not changed in over two-thousand years. Some of the words may change from one version to another. But the meaning is always the same."

"So then, how would you explain dinosaurs? They obviously lived years ago from scientific evidence, but the Bible doesn't mention them." I don't know if I asked because I want to know or if I was just testing her.

"Well, if God made everything in seven days, it only makes

sense that humans and dinosaurs lived at the same time. But you wouldn't find evidence of that now only because we are so fragile. We decay and turn into dust."

"What would have killed them all?"

"A flood. You see, God had Noah make the ark. It was made about thirty-feet tall with a top, middle, and lower section. The dinosaurs wouldn't have fit. If there is one thing we know about God, is that He has no problem sacrificing something for humans to live a better life."

"But—"

Maka barged into the room without warning.

She said something to him in a language didn't understand. I could tell she was irritated. Maka responded in what sounded like the same language. After a few minutes, Eve sighed. "We have to go with Maka."

I followed her.

Maka stopped at a few stores, but eventually dropped us off to babysit.

When we got to the house, as I'd predicted, the kids had already eaten pizza. Once the mothers left, I took my four kids outside to play. Eve stayed inside with the two babies. By ten o'clock, all the kids had fallen asleep on the living room floor watching *The Mask*. After the last kid had fallen asleep, I got up from the couch to find Eve in the kitchen, eating pizza. "Are the babies asleep?"

She nodded as she finished chewing. "I put them to sleep while you were cleaning up your kids."

A text came in on her phone. A big smile came across her face. "Donivan?" I asked.

"Mmhmm. He says that Damiano kept talking about you at the gym. That Leland got mad and did a number on him."

"They fought?" I asked, surprised.

"Not like that," she said quickly, after reading my expression. "Donivan says that the instructor saw it coming so he stuck them in a ring to duke it out."

I shrugged. "So, what's the deal between you and Bridget?"

"When we first moved here from Hawaii, we lived in a different district. We were good friends and she went to church with me a few times. Her father passed away. I did my best to talk to her about God, let her know that her father was in a better place." She paused. "Eventually, she stopped talking to me and started being rude to me. I just let her be."

"Are you sure that's it?"

"It was two years after I was in the eighth grade. I thought Bridget stopped talking to me because she was in high school. But about four weeks after my father passed away, I got off the bus and she was waiting at my bus stop. She came gave me a hug, took a step back and said 'Karma is a…' When I got to Moywood last year, a girl named Athena told me to steer clear of Bridget. That Bridget had been telling people that I was a home wrecker, a liar, and hypocritical." Eve kept talking, but the more she spoke, the angrier I got. Eve was the most kindhearted girl I'd ever known.

I was so lost in my thoughts that I didn't hear a knock on the door. I was startled when I realized Maka in front of me.

"You zone out a lot, huh?" he asked.

"No, I was just thinking."

"What did you do these past couple hours?"

"Hung out with Tim," Maka answered. "He's a cop. He's like my mentor. He goes to my church when his schedule allows."

We got back to Eve's house at about eleven-forty-five. By midnight, Eve and I were lying next to each other and neither of us could sleep. We talked about lighter subjects until finally falling asleep.

12

Eve and her mother took off for church while Maka drove me home.

"Don't you go to church?" I asked.

"Yes. I go to the night service. That service is just for the youth in grades sixth to twelfth. You're welcome to join me, if you would like."

"No, thank you. Tell me about Leland and Damiano."

Maka started laughing. "It was awesome. I wish I'd had a camera."

"What happened?"

"Dom for one reason or another kept bringing you up. So, Leland warned him to keep his mouth shut. Our instructor could see those two had friction, he told them to put the gloves on and put them in the ring. First round, they went blow for blow. Second round, Leland nails him with this one solid punch and knocks him out."

My mouth dropped. "Can he get in trouble for that?"

"No, I don't think so."

Maka started laughing again. "It was awesome."

When I got home, Mom was on the couch, writing again. "Oh,

Leona, sweetheart, I'm glad you're here. Would you mind painting my toenails like before? Your father and I are going to start going on our dates again."

Back in Maine, Mom and Dad would go on dates every other week. Mom always had me paint her nails. Every time she tried to do them herself, she would mess it up somehow.

"Do you want me to do it before I leave for my date?"

"Before would be best." Mom winked. "That way we can talk. I have my nail kit here when you're ready."

I dropped my things off in my room, took a shower, and got dressed. Passing Leland's room, I noticed he was still sleeping, so I ran and jumped on his bed. Jolted awake, he looked at me, then the clock. He closed his eyes again. "It's too early."

"Lee, its past ten." No response. "So, did you have to knock the guy out?"

His eyes stayed closed. "Who told you?"

"Donivan told Eve who told me. I asked Maka for details." I sighed. "You can't beat down every one that says my name."

"It was the *way* he did it. I don't like him. I made sure he knew it."

"Try not to do it again, okay? I don't want you to scare off any potentials."

"To hell with potentials. You don't need *potentials*."

All this attitude and his eyes were still closed. "Whatever you say." I moved toward the door. "I'll see you later. I have to do Mom's nails before my *date with Rodney*." I said the last in a sing-song voice to tease him.

"You have another date?" I looked back and Leland was looking at me, propped up on his elbows.

"Yes, I do. I'm leaving at noon." I went to the living room. "Okay, Mom, spread 'em." That's our inside joke. Mom can spread her toes like an oriental fan. When I first saw her do it, I tried it myself. I don't know why we were laughing so hard that day but I never did figure out how to spread my toes like she does. "What color did you pick?" She handed me a metallic-maroon color.

"So, tell me about your date. Is it with Baron?" She asked, still looking at her notepad.

"Of course it is."

"Don't say it like that. If you two aren't officially dating, then there is nothing wrong with dating someone else."

"I don't know Mom. I think I can only handle one guy at a time." I chuckled. "I think Leland and Dad can only handle one guy at a time."

Mom giggled. "You know honey, boys these days play games. They say, 'Don't hate the player, hate the game.' But really, it's up to the player to play the game." She paused. "This game they play is not a game that holds any kind of respect. What's worse is that a lot of girls fall for it. Women are just more emotionally involved than men. Because of that, sometimes we mistake lust for love."

"What's the difference?" I asked.

"Love is unconditional and is long lasting. Lust is blinding and temporary."

"So how do I tell the difference?"

"Time."

Somehow, I expected something a little more elaborate. "Duly noted."

Leland flopped down next to mom.

"Hey, watch it. Nail polish here." I gave Lee a stern look. He'd obviously never tried to get polish out of a sofa.

"Mom." Leland ignored me. "Why didn't we move to the house on Cape Cod?"

"Sweetheart, we don't need a house with seven bedrooms. It's just for the family to use when they wish."

"I say we use it this summer."

I raised my eyebrows.

He finished, barely able to contain his laughter. "Invite Rodney so we can go fishing and he can mysteriously go missing."

The bell rang, but when I went to answer it, Leland pushed me down and got it himself. Rodney walked in with Leland on his tail. I looked at the clock. Rodney was thirty minutes early.

"Good morning, Mrs. Sentmore. How are you?"

"I'm good, Baron, how are you?"

"I am doing well, thank you."

"Have a seat, Rodney," Lee said.

When Rodney sat on the love seat behind me, Leland took his seat next to mom.

Everyone was uncomfortably silent until my mother said, "Tell me, Baron, about the restaurant your family owns. Lucas and I are going out on a date tonight and we may want to go there."

"Oh, sure. All recipes are supposed to be from Louisiana. The restaurant itself is a jazz theme with jazz music playing. If you'd like, I could have them reserve you a table for seven-thirty."

"Oh, that would be great. Would you mind?"

"Not at all, Mrs. Sentmore." Rodney took out his cell phone and texted someone.

I looked up and noticed that Leland had not stopped glaring at him since he walked in. I hit his leg, but he didn't flinch. I put away the nail polish and stood.

Rodney puts away his phone. "You're all set, Mrs. Sentmore."

"Thank you, Baron."

"I'm ready to go," I said.

When Rodney stood, so did Leland. Leland brushed by me, putting something in my back pocket. Leland stood between Rodney and me.

"Do I have to remind you what my father said last week?" Leland asked.

Instead of answering Leland's question, Rodney said, "I heard about you and Dom at the gym."

"Keep that in mind when you take my sister out."

As I closed the door, I pretended to lock it to give me a moment to look at what Leland gave me. The knife again. I turned and Rodney was at the bottom of the porch steps waiting for me. When he wasn't looking, I tossed the knife in the bushes.

"What kind of music do you like?" he asked.

"Mostly RNB from, like, the nineties. Why?"

"We'll be on the road for about forty-five minutes. Maybe a bit longer."

"Oh, where are we going?"

"It's a surprise."

He stopped at a red light and looked at me. "I have some information I think you may like."

"Really?"

"I spoke to Brad about those art projects you were asking about. He said its an Israeli mermaid and that was the only thing she made a big deal about."

"What does Israel have to do with mermaids?" I asked. I pull out my phone and start to research Israel and mermaids. When all of a sudden, I heard the ringing for an outgoing call. It took me a moment to realize that the ringing was coming from the car speakers.

"Hello?"

"Hey Brad, its Rodney."

"Yeah, what's up?"

"Leona was asking about the mermaid thing."

"What about it?"

"Does she still have it?" I asked.

"No, she tossed it."

"What about a picture? Does she have a photo?"

"Not that I know of."

"Okay, last question. Do you know if it was in the school art show that year?"

"Yes. My mother made me go to the stupid thing," he said.

"Like you stayed very long." Rodney laughed.

"No way."

Finding It

Rodney chuckled, shaking his head. "Alright, Brad. I'll talk to you later."

I looked back down at my phone.

"What do mermaids have to do with Israel?" Rodney asked.

"It says the Israeli Government offers one-million dollars to anyone who can get a picture of a real mermaid."

"A million dollars for a picture?" Rodney asked.

"A million dollars for a picture. It looks like a few Americans supposedly caught one on video."

We kept talking about my findings, friends, family, school, and the vacation house. Before I knew it, we were turning off the highway. I noticed signs for a circus. "Are we going to a circus?"

"I thought it would be fun. Fried food, games, rides." He smiled.

After parking the car, we got in line for our tickets.

First, we ate. After we rode the rides and played some games, we were waiting in the line for the Ferris wheel.

"Are you having fun?" Rodney asked me.

"Yes, I am. I've never been to a circus before."

"Never?"

I shook my head.

We boarded the two-person cart. When the guy closed the restraint bar, Rodney reached to hold my hand. My heart began to race. Holding Rodney's hand, a part of me wanted to let go because I thought my hand might be sweaty. But if I pulled away, he'd think I don't want to hold his hand. Sweaty hands were so gross.

"I wanted to talk to you about something."

I stopped thinking about sweat.

"The next few months are going to be pretty busy for the family businesses. You know, because of the holidays. Anyways, I just want to give you a heads-up. I won't have much spare time on the weekends until about mid-January."

"Oh, okay," I said.

After the ride, time for more food. We'd just found seats near a group of very loud teenage boys, when I noticed they'd been throwing handfuls of popcorn at someone at another table. A girl at the other table seemed annoyed, but didn't say anything. I saw one of the boys trying to hide that he was unwrapping an ice cream cup. I walked toward him.

"Leona, what are you doing?" Rodney asked, grabbing my arm.

"Someone has to stop them." He was still holding my arm. "Let go of me, Rodney."

"It is none of our business," Rodney said.

"I'm making it my business." I tried to hand him my soda but it fell to the ground.

I saw two of the boys with their arms back, ready to throw something at the girl. I raced forward and knocked one of the things off course. Ice cream had landed on a girl. The one I intercepted had landed on one of the boys.

"Stanley, Don!" Someone behind me had yelled.

"You think that's funny, chick?" he asked, wiping the ice cream away.

"You seemed to think it was funny to throw ice cream on her." I nodded my head in the girl's direction.

"Stanley, Don!"

The kid took a step forward and I took a step back, bumping into the girl. Just then, Rodney stepped in front of me, shoving the boy.

"Back off, kid." he said.

Two other boys showed up. One was bald, the other had brown hair. Both showed enough muscles to lift a car. They started to usher the boys, Rodney included, away from the food area.

"You didn't have to do that," the girl said.

Then, a lady with little boy in a stroller walked into the section. "Hey, do you think you can spare a few wipes?" I showed the women my hand full of ice cream.

She looks at me and rummaged under the stroller for a moment. "Here." She handed me a pack of wipes. "You can keep them."

I sat down at the table and handed the girl a few wipes, then cleaned myself up.

The girl smiled. "What's your name?"

"Leona. What's yours?"

"Sarah."

She giggled. "Thanks."

When I found Rodney sitting on a bench, I apologized. We played a few more games, took a few pictures, and rode more rides.

I got home at eight-thirty. I almost panicked at the door again, but Rodney just gave me a kiss on the check. I wondered what he was waiting for.

I fell asleep thinking of everything that happened at the circus.

13

A month later... my days had become routine. Except for tomorrow – I leave for Hawaii, so exciting! I've been consistent with my homework and all my classes had a passing grade. Although, both Ms. Colner's music class and the meetings with Ms. Lumina were still a total waste of time.

After reviewing my progress report, I overheard my mother tell Dad that she felt like I'd only kept up my grades to go on the trip. I don't know what her issue was, but her persistent lack of faith in me... well it hurts. Last year was a long time ago.

Charley had texted Nick yesterday that he'd found what we were looking for and we'd see him today after school.

Rodney and I had been on two dates since the circus. We went to a Halloween party, which was fun until he gave me a drink called a Scooby Snack. He waited until I'd finished the drink to tell me that it had alcohol in it.

When we got to school, I went to my locker and Rodney was there. "Good morning."

"Hi." I smiled. "What's up?"

"I've come to say goodbye." He pulled something out of his pocket. "This is for you. A little something for you to remember me by while you're on your trip." He held up a key chain. Looking closer, I saw it had a slide show flashing with tiny pictures of us together and a few of just him.

I smiled. "Thank you. It's great."

"I'll miss you," he said, gliding his knuckles along my cheek. He leaned over and softly kissed my cheek. "Goodbye, beautiful." He walked away.

I unpacked my backpack into my locker.

"That was nauseating."

I didn't even have to look to know it was Nicolai behind me.

Ignoring his comment, I closed the locker door and turned to face him. "I'm going to your house this afternoon." I waited for him to say something, but he kept his eyes lowered while he rubbed the back of his neck. "You *promised*."

"Fine." He finally looked up. "I'll take you home on my way to work."

"Okay, be here after school so we can meet up with Charley together." He nodded and walked away.

Eve and I made it to our regular lunch table. As everyone was eating and talking, a boy seated a few tables away caught my attention. He was talking and gesturing exaggeratedly. A pair of boys walked toward him. As I watched, the guy waving his arms accidentally whacked one of the two as they reached his table. It seemed that the one sitting down was apologizing. But the guy who'd gotten hit seemed determined to fight.

On impulse, I strode over. "Hey man, I saw the whole thing. It was an accident. You should let it go."

The boy who'd been smacked was barely taller than me. Bushy, brown curly hair overshadowed his slim body. "You should min' yo own biz-ness." He spoke as if he had no sense of proper grammar. When he spoke, his index finger edged close to my face.

"Well, I'm a nosy woman." I was getting annoyed. "And I am makin' it my *biz-ness*." I mimicked his speech.

He took a small step closer. Now he was in my face. The boy

with the wild hands got up. Then Maka stepped between me and crazy hair. "Is there a problem here, Sam?" Maka asked him.

Sam, the aggressor, glanced behind me. I followed his gaze, only to see everyone at my table standing up, ready to jump into the anticipated fight.

"Nah, Maka, ain't no prob-um he-ya." He turned his eyes to me. "You know, you ain't da onliest one wit eyes fo' Rodney. If I wuz you, I be makin' sho he is alone ova da vacation." He bit his bottom lip and walked away.

When Sam was a good distance away, Maka grabbed my arm and marched me back to the table. "Your brother warned me you were a magnet for trouble."

I don't know which of their comments bugged me more.

After the last bell, I waited for Nick at my locker. When he finally showed, his face was as serious as ever. "Is something wrong?"

"When we go to my house... no matter how crazy it sounds, if I tell you to do something... just do it, okay?"

"Sure." I wondered what that meant.

We found Charley. I made sure I had the pictures in my back pocket. When we got to his house, Nick couldn't open the door. He knocked.

"Wait here." He disappeared around the corner of the house.

"What?" A woman yanked open the door. She had fresh makeup on, but still wore pajamas. "Who the hell are you?"

I could smell alcohol rolling off her in waves.

"I'm here for Nick," I said politely.

"He's not here." She raised her hand to close the door.

"Yes, I am, Ma." Nick caught the door before it slammed shut in my face. He grabbed my arm and pulled me in. His mother didn't say anything else.

We went into a bedroom.

"Hey angel, how was school?" Nick asked a little girl who was sitting on the bed.

"Good. Who's that?" She pointed at me.

"This is a friend from school. Her name is Leona. Leona, this is my little sister, Hayley."

We smiled and waved at each other awkwardly. Nick kneeled to talk to his sister. "Are you packed?" She shook her head. "Okay, go pack your bag. Also, bring your sight words and homework so we can go over it all in the shed."

She left the room. "I have to drop my sister off at my cousin's place. He watches her while I work." He took off his shirt and grabbed another.

"But your mom is home. Can't she watch her?"

He huffed. "The only thing that woman is good for is paying the bills and bringing a new guy home every week."

"Are you ready?" He saw Hayley standing by the door. When we walked through the living room, I saw Nick's mother on the couch. She had dressed and her hair was in a ponytail. She poured two glasses of wine and passed one to a man sitting close to her. We went through back door and into a shed in the backyard.

Nick sat on a stool in front of a desk. "The projects you want to see are over there, on the shelves." He pointed.

I went to look and I was flat-out amazed. I couldn't believe Mr. Littmen didn't grant him a perfect grade. The model of the Taj Mahal was stunning. It was well thought-out and constructed. You could tell that even assembling had been time consuming. I looked back at Nick. "You said that there were lights on it?"

"Yeah, it's battery operated. There's a switch on one of the corners." He turned back to his sister, who read a word from an index card.

I found the switch and flipped it. After examining the piece, I looked up to see a deep-blue box. It was a graveyard of four or five sunken ships and a few wrecked planes. I flipped its switch and a dim light illuminated the inside of the box. "Is this the Bermuda box you were talking about?"

"I can't believe he didn't give you the grade," I said, switching off the lights. I took the envelope from my back pocket and tossed it onto the desk. "Would you like to open it?"

"Yes, I would." Nick grabbed the envelope.

"How old are you?" I asked Hayley.

"Seven."

"Whoa." Nick's eyes widened.

I looked at the picture. "Freaky, right?"

"What is that?" Nick turned the picture as if would help him focus.

"It's a mermaid. The Israeli government offers a million dollars for a picture of a mermaid people reportedly have seen."

"Somehow, I thought mermaids looked like Ariel and her sisters."

The sculpture had a big black eye that reminded me of anime characters' eyes, but it was completely black. A fin ran down the center of its head. Shredded money made up the scales on the tail. The hands were webbed and had claws. It sat on a rock. At the base of the rock was a small card with the one sentence that explained the sculpture.

"I don't see how that is grade worthy. *Three plus one is?*"

"Four." Hayley answered.

Nick was right. "When you think of Israel, what's a few things that come to mind?"

"Christianity, Muslim, and Jews. Two subtract two."

Hayley looked down at her fingers, mentally doing the math. "Zero."

"Maybe that's why Mr. Littmen liked it so much. Anyone else would have handed in the obvious. Who would have thought to turn in a million-dollar mermaid?"

"Maybe." He looked at his watch. "We have to go."

When we got to his car, someone had parked behind him. Annoyed, he went and hit the hood of the Mazda way too hard for comfort. "Stop sucking on my mom's face and move the car so I can get to work," he yelled.

Finding It

The man came out, opened the driver's door and stood there. "Hit my car like that again, you and I are going to have a problem. You hear me, son?"

I'd moved to push Nick back to his own car. He didn't move an inch.

I heard Nick's mom holler, "Rob, get back into the car. I'll handle my son."

Nick looked me straight in the eye. "Get in the car."

"Nikki." His mother spoke.

I stepped around his mother and took a few steps but stopped short of the passenger door.

"What are you doing? Are you trying to ruin this for me?" She sounded old and tired.

"Ruin what, Ma? By next week, you'll have a new man that you'll swear is better than the last thirty you've had."

She slapped Nicolai across the face. "Don't you talk to me like that, Nicolai Coverdale. I am *still* your mother."

He leaned toward her and spoke quietly. Then he moved to his car. He noticed I was still standing there. My eyes bugged out.

"I told you to get in the car."

We both got in and, boy, was it quiet. After a few minutes, we turned into an apartment complex called Coverdale Apartments. "Does your cousin own the apartment complex?"

"Andrew does, Chase just lives here," Nicolai answered.

We parked in front of the leasing office and went to the apartment on the right. The man who opened the door was at least five-inches taller than Nicolai. He looks like he ate well and worked out, too. He had the same dirty-blonde hair as Nicolai.

After the initial *hello,* Nick introduced me. "Chase, this is my friend from school, Leona. Leona, my cousin, Chase."

"It's nice to meet you." We shook hands.

"Come on in." A skinny woman had picked up and was hugging Hayley. "Leona, this is my girlfriend, Luna."

"Es nice to mee you." She spoke with a heavy Spanish accent.

"Nice to meet you, too."

She looked back at Hayley. "Mamita, go put your stuff in the room and wash you hans."

When Hayley left, we had a seat in the living room. "You're going to want to talk to her before she goes to bed tonight," Nick said.

"Another run-in with your mother?" Chase asked.

Nicolai sighed.

"What happened?"

Nicolai recapped the incident and Luna listened from the kitchen. When Nick finished, Chase looked at me. "You met a Coverdale sister."

I nodded, having no words.

"I'm sorry," he said. "You'll have nightmares tonight, too."

After a few minutes Nick said, "We gotta go."

He drove me home and the conversation stayed casual.

Maka and Eve were waiting for me. We grabbed my things and my father gave me the prepaid debit card with four-hundred and twenty dollars on it.

Later, on Eve's bed, I was too excited to sleep. "It's past eleven o'clock. Should we try and get some sleep?"

"No, it's only five in the evening in Hawaii. We are going to have to adjust the times we sleep, anyway. We might as well start now."

"Okay.... how's Donivan?"

I could see her blush, even in the dim light.

"Good." Her voice squeaked.

"Have you gone on a date yet?"

"Well, the youth group went bowling a few weeks ago. We hung out then, but we haven't gone a one-on-one date yet." She sounded disappointed. "You and Rodney do anything interesting?"

"Not really. We went to a circus and almost got into a fight."

Eve propped herself up on an elbow. "I was actually asking if he's kissed you or not. But you can tell me about the circus. That sounds interesting."

I told her the story. When I finished, she looked completely dumbfounded. "What would possess you to go up against five teenage boys?"

I shrugged.

"What were you thinking when you tried to stand up for Dathon?"

"Who?" I asked.

"Dathon Lukash, the boy waving his arms at lunch."

"Oh. the only thing I know for sure is that I was grateful for Maka and his friends. I don't even—"

A knock at the bedroom door interrupted me.

"Come in," Eve said.

The door opened and Maka came in. "Do you mind if I join you? Staying up on your own is hard to do."

"It's up to Leona."

"Sure, why not?"

Eve flipped the lamp back on. Clearly, no sleep was coming anytime soon.

"So, what are you two talking about?" He straddled a chair, sitting backwards, resting his arms on the top.

"About how grateful I am to have a group of beefy-fighter friends," I said, jokingly.

He shook his head. "What were you thinking?"

"I don't know." I paused. "I saw the way that one guy was acting... so aggressive. I just... went over."

"Well, going up against Sam is a sure way to get hit," Eve said.

"What do you mean?"

"Sam is from Flint, Michigan. He has no problem hitting people if they'll steer clear of him later," Eve answered.

"Well, the one sitting down looked like he needed a little help."

"Dathon was most likely avoiding a fight with his mother more than avoiding a fight with Sam," Maka said. "His mother is a cop for the Woodstock Police Department." He chuckled. "Imagine a call coming over the dispatch radio, "Officer Lukash, your son got into a fight at school and needs to be picked up." She'd stuff him in the back seat like a criminal, she'd be so mad." He chuckled again.

"Sounds like you are talking from experience. Maka, have you ever been suspended?" I teased.

"Yes, he has," Eve said. "Freshmen year – for fighting."

"No way. Who'd you fight?"

"Sam." Maka answered.

"You're kidding."

"Sam and I were arguing. He said something that ticked me off and I hit him." He shrugged. "Even though I was fifteen and taller than my mom, she came to the office, grabbed my ear and twisted it like I was a kid. She held on until I got in the car. It still hurts when it rains." He rubbed his right ear and grinned.

I laughed so hard I fell over on the bed.

"At home she yelled for another hour."

We kept talking until Mrs. Aquino came into the room to tell us to start getting ready. We all fell asleep on the drive to the airport.

14

By the time we got to Kaua'I, we were exhausted. It took two hours to get settled and eat. When I finally laid my head down, I was asleep immediately.

On Sunday, I was in the bathroom getting ready for church. I opened the bathroom door and asked Eve, "Does this look okay?" I wore a summer dress with a purple, green, and yellow abstract design.

"You look great." She had on a white fifties-era dress with black polka dots and blue yellow and green flowers.

We were going to pick up her grandmother before church. It only took moments to get there. Maka went to the front door. A little old lady came out. She was about the same height as Mrs. Aquino, but skinnier. Her skin was paler than the rest of the Aquinos. In fact, she didn't even look related. "She's your grandmother?" I asked.

"Biologically no, but she's been a friend of the family so long, we just call her that," Eve said.

"Why is Maka walking with her that way?" Maka held her left hand, his right was at the small of her back as he walked alongside.

"She's blind, sweetheart," Mrs. Aquino told me.

"And how are you, Kai?" She settled into the car.

"I'm doing good, Grandma Sue. How are you?" Eve answered.

"Warmer than you," she joked. "We have an extra person in the car. What's your name, beautiful?"

Eve elbowed me, letting me know the question was for me. I looked to the front seat. The old woman was looking up at the ceiling of the car waiting for my response. "My name is Leona."

"You can call me Grandma Sue. Tell me, Leona, are you enjoying yourself?"

I hesitated to answer. "Ummm, I haven't seen much. We've only been here two days, but I think I could get used to the weather."

"Well I'm glad you're starting your trip here with church. You're a very stubborn woman, but not too stubborn for the Lord."

My eyebrows shot up in surprise. "Okay."

We got to the church and a plethora of people greeted us with smiles, hugs, and kisses to the cheek. People greeted me with a *God bless you* and I didn't know how to respond.

Finally, we found seats the eighth row from the front. I looked down at my book and began reading.

Shortly after, people sang a few songs. I listened while the pastor spoke.

"Who knows? Maybe you just never seemed to fit in. Here's why. Because you were never supposed to fit in. It says, in Romans twelve-two, 'Do not conform to the patterns of this world.' Because the ways of the world are backwards. We are in the end of days, where what is wrong is being called *right*. You know what's funny? When we were younger, all we wanted was to fit in. Then when we get older, all we want is to do something that will set us apart. So, if you're young, trying to figure out why you have never quite fit in, I beg you stop. Because later, you're going to want to undo that fitting-in thing. You were *meant* to be set apart. You were *meant* to stand out. It's nice to have people like you. To have people you can call friends. Yes, that is nice. But it's not always what others may think. Like people who are famous. They have more people than a whole country *liking them* and, because of that, they can't go on vacation without someone snapping their picture. They can't have a family dilemma without it ending up in the tabloids. They can't even mourn a death of a loved one without someone checking out what they wore to the funeral and how much their clothes cost. Fitting in and being liked is overrated. Do what God called you to do and you won't have to worry about any of that. You..."

I stopped listening.

After church, we headed home, stopping to drop off Grandma Sue.

"I would like Leona to walk me to the door. If you don't mind."

I tried holding her hand and back the way Maka had earlier.

"Leona, I know you don't believe in Jesus yet, but He is real. He saves people now just as much as he did back on the cross of Calvary. He'll show Himself to you, if you would just pay attention."

"With all due respect, Grandma Sue, I don't really believe in anything. How can I pay attention to something I'm not looking for?"

"Ah, well it is possible. You see, God has sent His only Son to die on the cross. He took with Him all of our sins. Three days later, He redeemed us all. If you ever confess to believing that, your life would change forever. It's a beautiful truth. But for now, God would like to protect you."

We reached the front door and she turned to face me.

"How would God protect me?" I asked in a quiet voice.

"You would just have to listen to Him."

"And what would He be saying?"

"That the gentleman on your keychain is no good. You should do away with him."

My heart skipped a beat. How on earth would this woman

know about that? Or Rodney? I hadn't even shown Eve the keychain.

"You are the mountain only God can move. He's working on you, little lady. God bless you." She opened her door and was gone.

On the way back to the car, I thought about what just happened but tried to shake it off.

In the car, Eve asked, "Are you okay?"

I pursed my lips. "Your Grandma Sue freaks me out." *If there was a God, He was going to have a hard time moving me.*

Back at the house, Maka said, "Hey, Leona, change into shorts and sneakers. Pack a small bag with a bathing suit and your camera. After we eat, I'll take you to my getaway."

I HIKED BEHIND MAKA. We stopped periodically to take pictures. Like, when I saw a pineapple plant. I thought pineapples grew on trees. Maka laughed at my amazement. The trail we were on sloped downhill and ended up at a lake. I realized that we had walked down the side of a beautiful waterfall. We were completely surrounded by trees and rocks that formed the cliff for the waterfall.

"How did you find this place?" I asked.

"It's part of the perks of living on the island. As a boy, you get bored and just wander in the woods. One of my buddies knew of this place. We wandered off to find it."

"It's beautiful." I snapped a few pictures.

It wasn't long before some of Maka's friends joined us. I snapped a few photos of his friend who had gotten a tatau done. One of them let me to borrow an underwater camera, he said I was going to need it. I don't know how long we were there, but I took plenty of pictures. At some point, Maka took my phone and camera and threw me in the water.

15

It's been four days of nothing but sightseeing. Eve took me scuba diving. I struggled to get into the wet suit and needed help. Eve showed me how to put it on in thirty seconds. Afterwards, we went with Mrs. Aquino to feed the homeless. Tuesday and Wednesday, I spent most of the day taking pictures and studying the flowers in Mrs. Aquino's garden. Then she took me to meet a few of her friends and went surfing. I wore myself out trying to master it, so ended up sitting on the board at the surf break, just taking pictures of everyone else. When sunset came, everyone stopped surfing and sat on their boards watching the sunset. I got a little nervous sitting in the dark, open water but I got beautiful pictures.

Today, Eve's aunt was coming. Mrs. Aquino says her sister got permission to take us to her workplace. Eve told me about her last night; their aunt was single, had no kids and didn't go to church. I was grateful. I think I had heard enough of *Jesus loves you* for one vacation. I mean, I got they wanted to share the love, but I'd told them multiple times that I wasn't interested.

While we were waiting, Rodney texted me saying he missed me. I told him that if there wasn't so much beauty here in Hawaii, I would probably miss him, too. He called a few minutes later. I told him the keychain kept me from missing home. After we hung up, he texted me a kiss emoji. It made my heart jump. Call me stupid, but that was our first kiss.

Eve's aunt gets to the house at one in the afternoon. She introduced herself as Kiki. Maka, Eve, and I piled into the car. Kiki explained that she was a nurse. Where she worked, they'd started a program to help keep kids in line. She said she wanted us to see for ourselves.

In the parking lot, a sign read: *Never Give Up Rehab Center*. We followed her to a front desk. The lady there gave us each a visitor's sticker. "You will be meeting three people today," Kiki said.

We walked down a corridor similar to a hotel. We turned into a room where a woman laid in a hospital bed. Looking at her, I decided I would rather have gone to church.

"This is Zuleka," Kiki said. "She is twenty-nine years old and has been here for four years. Zuleka, these are three students in the Line Up Program, would you like to tell them your story?"

The woman looked us over. "I was twenty-five years old and finally graduating with a law degree. A few friends and I decided the day before we walk across the stage was a good day to just... party it out." Her eyes misted over with memories. "We'd all had plenty to drink. But when it was rehearsal time, no one wanted to miss it. You'd think that one of us who'd just earned a degree – in law, no less – would have known to call a cab. But we took two cars and drove off. I was in the second car. The first car swerved, for whatever reason, and somehow t-boned ours. We end up flipping over, right into a ditch. I sat behind the driver, the only one in my car wearing a seat belt. Out of the eight in that car wreck, only three survived. I can move only my arms and head. What's sad is not being paralyzed, but that I knew better."

The still-raw emotion of the woman affected everyone. Nobody moved.

"I am one of the fortunate ones, still able to work. The guy who drove the first car opened a law firm. I take his calls while he's in court. I realize that things could have been far worse."

Kiki said, "Thank you, Zuleka. Does anyone have a question?"

We shook our heads.

"Okay, on to our next person."

I tried to prepare myself for whatever could be next.

"This is Tim," Kiki said. "Tim, these three teens are a part of the Line Up Program... may I tell them your story?" He blinked twice. "Tim was the captain of his high school football team. He made straight As and had a free ride to FSU. Prom night, he tried a drug that made him think he could jump from the roof of a building. Now, he can't walk or talk. He eats through this tube." Kiki lifted the blanket, showing us a tube connected to his stomach. "His only way of communicating is by blinking. He blinks once for *no* and twice for *yes*."

I found myself standing next to Tim. "Hi, Tim. My name is Leona. I don't... well, I just wanted to wish you a Happy Thanksgiving." I watched him and he blinked three times.

"He said 'thank you,'" Kiki said. Tim's eyes turned teary. "Thank you for your story Tim." In the next room, we saw a man in a wheelchair. "This is Harry. He tried heroin and crashed his car. A pole hit his head so hard that they had no choice but to remove that part of the skull and brain."

It was then that I noticed a dent in his head. His hair covered it up pretty well. "His mind stays stuck in time. If you ask him how old he is, he will say he's nine. He can't walk, but he can feed himself. Are you okay, Kai?"

Eve was pale and looked about ready to vomit.

"Let's go sit in the lobby."

In the lobby, we sat on a large couch. Kiki gave Eve some water.

"Like Zuleka said, the shame is not what happened to them, but that they all knew better. Maka, you're a junior." Her head swiveled to Eve and me. "You two are sophomores. Life doesn't stop after high school. There is so much more to live for. Don't think you can party or try someone just once without any consequences. Just think of these people before you do anything as simple as having a beer. Or trying a pill. Be smart and think about what you're doing."

Back at the house, we sat in the living room discussing the day. Saturday, before we left, we spent most of the day relaxing. By six-thirty, Eve had frantically rummaged through everything.

"Leona was such a sweetheart to the second guy. That was so considerate. It would have been more touching if Eve hadn't gotten sick." Maka finished with a grin.

"Hey," Eve protested. "I just turned a bit green."

"All I did was say *happy Thanksgiving*," I mumbled.

"But how many people, other than nurses, actually said that to him?" Maka asked.

"Okay, whatever."

Mrs. Aquino cleared her throat. "They're only saying you have a beautiful heart."

"I got it. Thanks for the compliment."

Eve stood and went from one room to another, apparently searching. Mrs. Aquino went to help her.

Maka whispered, "Eve is supposed to take you to a live luau. Fire and everything."

"Really?"

"Really."

"There's fire at a luau?"

He nodded. "Sometimes." After a moment, Maka said, "I wanted to apologize for one of my friends. Polunu says one of the guys was rude about showing you his tatau. He said that it seemed like he purposely stood around, just so he could refuse to show you, before jumping in the water."

I thought back to the day at the waterfall. "I don't know that he was being rude. I could tell he has a chip on his shoulder, but I doubt it was about me."

"Not directly to you, but people from the mainland. Keli'I believes that our culture is dying. Instead of just holding onto the

Finding It

culture, he blames America and interracial marriage. Says Pearl Harbor would have never happened if America wouldn't have bought Hawaii. He thinks people should stick to their own kind."

"Stick to their own kind?" I raised my eyebrows.

Maka slowly nodded.

"Wow." *What can you say to something like that?* "Do you agree with him?"

"No. Yes, culture is dying, but if America hadn't bought Hawaii, someone else would have. There are people who were born and raised here that don't follow our culture. As far as interracial marriages, you can't help who you fall in love with. God sets people up according to compatibility and morality, not race. If I marry someone from the mainland, I'll be sure my kids are taught my culture. Let them choose their path when they've grown."

Eve rushed past, heading outdoors.

"I read an article a while back about people saying interracial marriages were against God's plan."

"Well, I have heard of that. But, every time God told a tribe of Israel not to marry from another tribe or whatever, it was because they had a different *religion*. I think God was more trying to keep them from idolatry, not from interracial marriages."

"Remind me never to debate the Bible with you."

He laughed. "I have read it a few times."

"I found them!" Eve screamed, as she burst through the door, waving tickets.

So, I got to go to a real luau. There were four people playing instruments and singing. The first two dancers were women. They wore solid red tank tops and red skirts with black and white flowers at the hem. They had what looked like a feather belt that that went around their hips, each ankle, each wrist, and as a crown on their heads. The hula they did was very graceful. Their second dance was faster but still graceful.

Then, children danced. They were the cutest things. I expected someone to mess up, but they were perfect.

The men made me unconformable. All they wore was what looked like oversized, puffy diapers made of green cloth. They stomped and pounded their chests. It seemed like a dance of dominancy.

16

Back on the mainland, Rodney had been over and met the family. Logan didn't like Rodney as soon as he met him. I've noticed every time Rodney and I were together he'd managed to find a reason to drink. I was starting to wonder whether he ever drank plain water. But no one was perfect and I couldn't expect anyone to put up with my flaws if I wasn't willing to deal with theirs.

Nick and Hayley spent Christmas dinner with us and were joining us for New Year's Eve.

In my room, I was working on something for art. I had two wooden boards upright and a baseboard, creating a corner. I wanted to create two shelves that could swivel out. Each shelf shows a negative thing about Hawaii. When they open, they show the beautiful waterfall and a beach with flowers. I already texted Nick for help.

A knock on my bedroom door interrupted my thoughts. "Come in." Then, I realized it was Greg. I opened the door. "Come in," I signed to him.

"Hey, can I talk to you?"

"Sure."

"What is you boyfriend's name?"

"Rodney." I finger-spelled the name.

"I don't like him." Greg didn't hesitate.

"You don't know him."

"No, not really. But something about him isn't right. I don't know how to explain it."

"You probably talked to Logan."

"Logan doesn't like him, either?"

I shook my head.

"Men know men. If more than one man says they don't like the guy, you should probably listen."

Remembering what Grandma Sue said back in Hawaii made me stop and think. But a group of us had already started making plans for spring break. Since Leland and my parents would be out of town, I was going to be at home alone. Rodney, four other people and I had started making plans to go to the vacation home in Massachusetts. Logan and Emily were going to meet us there and be our chaperones. Mom and Dad reluctantly approved.

"Greg, I appreciate your concern, but I'll be fine. Thank you."

"Okay," He signed. "Can I help you with anything?" He pointed to my project.

"Not really. Nick is going to take a look at it."

"He seems like a good person. But he also looks like he has a heavy load on his shoulders."

I hated to admit it, but Greg got that right. "Yeah, he's a good person but has got a lot going on at home."

Greg smiled. "Nick would be the one I would tell you to date."

I looked at him with an arched eyebrow. He put his hands up to imply he'd surrendered.

Nick and Hayley should be here soon. The Aquino family will be here, too. Rodney had to work but would stop by. Our family tradition was to spend the night playing board games and, when midnight comes, we went around the room to each person and

Finding It

shared our highlights of the past year and goals for the year to come.

Dinner was ready. I got a text from Rodney saying that he got called into work early and wouldn't be stopping by. I texted back, "Ok."

At 11:50pm, we had played Boggle, Scrabble, Taboo, Yahtzee, Trouble, Family Feud, Clue, and Life.

The clock struck midnight.

First Mom shared. "My highlight I would have to say is the move. Because of the move, I met Moana. I feel like you are the sister I never had. I'm grateful." Mrs. Aquino smiled. "My goal is to finish this book and at least one other."

Next was Logan. "Well, I think this would fall into both categories." Then he kneeled down on one knee with a ring in his hand. I gasped. "Emily, you are everything I have waited for. Please make me the happiest man in the world by saying *yes* to becoming my wife."

"Yes," she said, in tears.

We all clapped. The guys congratulated them. The girls hugged, on the verge of tears. When everyone settled down, it was Emily's turn. "I can't think of anything but Logan being a part of my life. You two did a great job raising him. He's the gentleman every woman dreams of having. That's all I've got."

After Mrs. Aquino spoke. Then it was Maka, Leland, Greg, Eve, and Nick. Nick was the one that surprised me the most. "I'm grateful to have Leona as a friend. You have a tender heart and, despite the guards you have up, you have shown me that I could have something to look forward to. That life isn't always a downward slope to nothing. Last year was a bad year, but my goal is to make next year better."

My turn. "I have to say that last year had a handful of bad and a handful of good. Aside from actually finding a few friends..." I hated it, but I was getting emotional. I cleared my throat. "So, I think I found something I was missing. I mean I feel like I don't know... I...." Inhaling, I changed the subject. "But I will say the best highlight of the year was going to Hawaii." Everyone chuckled. "My goal is to get my perfect grade."

Dad finished up the tradition and everyone was done for the night. I walked with Nick to his car. He was carrying Hayley, who had fallen asleep earlier. "I'm sorry if I made you uncomfortable when we took turns and stuff."

"Yeah, you did a little."

"Sorry, I wasn't trying to imply that I liked you or anything. But you said you came from a destructive year last year. You seem to have a grip on things now. I don't know... I hope to get to that point soon."

"I hope so too, Nick. You've been dealt a bad hand. Maybe you can learn to bluff your way into a jackpot." I got distracted by the view of Rodney's truck driving up.

He hopped out of the truck and walked over. "What's going on?"

"I'll see you around, Leona." Nick got into his car and drove off.

"Rodney, I thought you weren't coming."

He handed me a thin, glass tube.

"A shot for the new year." We tapped the two tubes together and drank it. Then he pulled out another two from his pocket. "These are for our upcoming spring break trip. It'll be full of adventures and moments to remember." I took the second one. I almost expected him to pull more out of his pocket, but instead he cradled my chin between his index finger and thumb and planted a soft kiss on my lips.

"Leona."

Hearing a gruff voice, I turned and saw Logan. My heart raced. I hope he didn't see me drinking the liquor.

"I thought you said he wouldn't be stopping by tonight."

"He just pulled up. I didn't know he was still coming," I said.

"Yeah man, it was a last minute thing. I was just wishing her a happy New Year." Rodney said.

"With two shots?" Logan asked.

I inhaled and I lashed out. "Logan, you're not Dad. So, you can either leave us alone or go tell Dad."

"No, I'm not Dad but watching how quickly you took those two shots, I can tell it wasn't you first time drinking with him. So, I am going to say this once to both of you." Logan turned to Rodney. "*You*. I don't like you. I don't want you around at all. For the rest of the time that I'm here, don't come over."

I rolled my eyes.

"If a man has to give you two shots before giving you a kiss, he isn't worth your time. You have three minutes to come inside." Logan sounded a lot like Dad.

"When is he leaving?" Rodney asked.

"Not for another three days."

"Don't be surprised if I come knocking at you bedroom window just to see you." He winked.

"Goodnight, Rodney." I smiled.

He kissed me again and left.

I tried to head straight to bed but Logan was in the living room waiting. I stood with my arms crossed, waiting for him to say something.

"Was he the one to give you your first drink?" he asked quietly.

There was no sense in lying. "Yes."

"I don't know how long you've been drinking, but I hope you stop now, before it becomes an addiction."

"Oh, come on Logan. You drink. Are you really in a position to tell me to stop?"

"I did drink, yes, freshmen year in college. But ask me how hard it was to stop drinking. Leona, things like alcohol and smoking cigarettes may not seem like a big deal because you're only drinking occasionally. But then you realize you can't go a weekend without it."

"Are you going to be this way during spring break?"

"No. Chances are, if you don't take my advice now, then you won't take it later. If you guys choose to drink during spring break, you'll sneak around and do it whether I tell you to or not. Just don't let Emily or me see you."

"Fine. Are we done?" He was being sensible and I was having a hard time staying mad.

"I only have one question."

I raised my eyebrows.

"Is losing ten-grand worth a few drinks?" he asked, referring to the money in my savings account.

"I'll only loose the ten-grand if I get caught."

"Goodnight, Leona." He sounded disappointed.

When I got into bed, I realized something. I hadn't gone a weekend this month without drinking some sort of alcohol. I wonder if that made me an addict.

17

I didn't even have art today, but Nick said he'd finished his half and my part was ready, so we're turning it in. We'd been working on it nonstop. We hadn't even handed in any other artwork just to finish this. Nick built the two shelves to swivel out. On the top shelf, I made a scene to represent when we fed the homeless. On the second shelf, I sculpted a few things and covered it with fake money and dollar-sign confetti to show the expensive cost of living there. Nick added lights and something behind the waterfall and under the beach to make it look like moving water. I sculpted two girls dancing the hula. Nick made them slowly sway back and forth.

I covered the project and walked with Nick. It took both of us to carry it. We sat it next to Mr. Littmen's desk. Nick left and I turned to Mr. Littmen. "This is my entry for the challenge."

"Okay. Is there anything I should know about it?"

"Just flip the switch."

"All right."

I walked out of the room and was a nervous wreck the rest of the morning. Eve even offered to pray for me when I got to English class. We got interrupted by the intercom. "Mr. Warren?"

"Yes?"

"Do you have Leona Sentmore in your class?"

My heart dropped at the sound of my name coming through the intercom.

"Yes, I do."

"Could you please have her go to Mr. Littmen's class? He would like to speak with her."

Mr. Warren handed me a pass. I wondered if I was in trouble. I texted Nick on the way to let him know that I'd been called to the art room.

Mr. Littmen was leaning over my project.

"Yes, sir?"

"Leona Sentmore, you are truly a determined individual." He flipped the switch off and sat at his desk. His eyes were red, as if he had been crying. "I can see Mr. Coverdale's hand in this project. Did he help you with it?"

"Yes, sir. But he only did what I had asked him to do. I wouldn't have been able to finish the project otherwise." I could hardly stand still.

"The falls and ocean move at the right pace. But what really caught me was the detail with the people and in the flowers. The homeless people and the money." He stopped talking and began to cry.

"Why are you crying?" I was horrified.

"You see, Leona, I just last night had been praying to God because I felt like my heart may had turned from flesh back into stone. Your reminded me of a time when I was homeless. When I finally got a job, I became so attached to money that I lost myself." He paused, just breathing. "Then when I opened the two shelves, it reminded me of when I finally looked at God and found, not only freedom, but beauty."

I was thoroughly confused.

He continued, "I know that that isn't what you were meaning to imply with your project, but it spoke to me. I didn't expect for God to use a student's artwork to speak to me, but He did. Congratulations, Leona. You got your grade."

I couldn't talk for a moment. "I... I got the grade?"

He laughed. "But I will be rewarding Mr. Coverdale as well. From now on, you and Mr. Coverdale will be required to hand in one piece every week. Your work will not be graded, but Mr. Coverdale's work will be. Sign this paper please, so I can put it in the art show at the end of the year. You can go back to class." He called the office and requested Nick.

On my way back to class, I texted Eve and Rodney to let them know I won the grade. Eve sent back a bunch of smiley faces. Rodney asked for my locker combination. He said he had to leave school early but would leave something in my locker to congratulate me with.

Sure enough, when I checked my locker, there was a Snapple bottle inside with a small Post-it note that said, "DO NOT SHARE ME." I took a sip and, just as I suspected, it was spiked.

When I got home, mom was waiting for me in the living room with Moana. They both hugged and congratulated me. We were all to be eating dinner together. Shortly after, Eve and Maka walked through the door. Dad was working late, so we ate without him.

"When is the art show?" Moana asked.

"The paper I signed said it would be May twentieth."

When we finished dinner, we all went to our own little corners. Eve came with me to my room.

"Oh, here." Eve handed me a plain envelope. "Don't open it now. Just open it whenever you feel like it." I put it in the top drawer of my desk. "How are things going with you and Rodney?"

"Fine. But I suppose it would be. We've only been together a little over a month. We haven't really gone anywhere, actually. What about you and Donivan? Are things still at a standstill?"

"We are still just talking," Eve said.

"What are you guys waiting for?" I asked.

"We are waiting on God."

"Seriously?" She nodded. "What is God going to do, come down on a cloud and say *get married*?"

"No," she said bashfully. "We just want to make sure that feelings won't get in the way of what God has planned for our lives. Many people get married with an option of divorce. When I get married, there will only be one way out and it won't be with a paper."

I heard a knock on the door. "Come in."

"Congratulations, honey," my dad said, walking in.

"Thanks, Dad."

"Eve, your mom says they're leaving."

Today was a good day.

18

When we first got to the house for spring break, Logan acted annoying about Rodney and me. I was sleeping on the ground floor and the rest of the group slept on the second floor.

We'd gone whale watching, to Providence Town during the day and at night. We've gone to Nantucket, Martha's Vineyard, to the mall, and the movies.

May and Brandy annoy me. Ethan and Zack pretty much left me alone, except for yesterday, when Zack decided to steal from a 7-Eleven. We went to the beach last night and wanted to have a bonfire. We sent Zack to get wood.

Then the cops showed up to tell us no bonfires were allowed and the beach was closed. Then, they kept us from leaving because they'd identified Zack and Rodney's car as the one that left the 7-Eleven. Zack had stolen the wood. Luckily, the alcohol had been mixed with juice in Hawaiian Punch bottles. We had exhausted our supply anyway. Rodney was the one who saved us. He volunteered to pay for the stolen wood and they let us go after they took him and Zack to the 7-Eleven to pay for it. We were lucky they didn't breathalyzer test us. We would have all failed.

Next morning, everyone left to go see the Kennedy's compound.

I'd already seen it. Plus, Rodney and I were up most of the night talking on the phone. The plan for tomorrow was to go to Salem where they'd held the famous witch trials. Meaning, they killed everyone who'd been accused.

I'd just woken up and spotted Emily and Logan on the love seat. "Should you two be sitting so close?" I joked, squeezing myself in.

"Well, good morning to you," Logan responded.

"I heard your friends left early this morning," Emily said.

"Yeah they wanted to see where the Kennedys live."

"You said that was off limits to the public," Emily said.

"It's supposed to be."

"I told them that, but I think they plan on parking at one of the nearby beaches and walking close enough to see the houses."

"I won't be bailing them out if they get in trouble," Logan said. "Rodney went with them?"

"I suppose so."

"Is that the kind of man you want to be with?" Logan said sarcastically.

"We need to start getting ready." Emily said, trying to keep the peace.

"Where are you going?" I asked.

"We are going to walk Main Street in Hyannis," Emily said. Logan went into another room. She leaned close to me. "I think Rodney is still upstairs," she whispered. "I'm going to try to get Logan to go the mall, but he doesn't want to. I'll text you when we're on our way back."

I went to my room and texted Rodney. "Did you go to the compound?"

It took a few minutes, but he responded with *no*. I filled him in with what was going on and how we would be by ourselves soon. I told him that I would call him when the coast was clear.

After they left, I called Rodney and started cooking breakfast. We ate and played an old Super Nintendo game. We watched a few movies in his room and fell asleep in each other's arms at the beginning of the second movie.

I woke up to the sound of a car door closing. My heart dropped when I heard Logan's voice. I checked my phone. Past six at night. Emily had texted about fifty minutes ago.

"Oh God."

"What?" Rodney said, half asleep.

"Logan is home," I whispered.

"Okay. Just relax. Just stay up here and when you're ready to go down, text what's-her-face to distract him while you sneak back downstairs."

"How are you so calm?" I whispered, slightly frustrated.

"Because there isn't much we can do. You are either going to get caught or you're not. Just deal with it when that time comes."

"That time has come Rodney. That time is right now."

"No," He whined and pulled me back down onto the bed. "Just cuddle with me more. Take advantage of the fact that you can't go downstairs yet."

"It has been nice cuddling." I laid back down.

"You are so beautiful." He kissed me.

After a few moments of kissing, his hands started to wander. I hesitated on whether I wanted to stop him or not, but before I had a chance to make up my mind, he shifted himself and was on top of me. I panicked. This had never happened and I didn't know what to do. His kisses moved from my lips to my neck.

I gasped, "I don't want to do this."

"Trust me," he said. "You'll enjoy it."

I felt his weight bear down on my hip.

I gasped again and said, "If you don't stop, I'll scream *rape* and my brother is right downstairs."

He lifted up his head. "Are you serious?"

I poked him in the eye. He rolled on his side, covering his eye in pain. I scurried off the bed and stood by the door and repeated myself. "*I said* I don't want to do this, Rodney."

He sat up. "We're in a room by ourselves... what did you think was going to happen?"

"What?"

"I have been putting up with you for four months now. I won't stick around if you aren't going to put out. No girl is worth the waiting for."

I desperately tried to process everything that had just happened and everything he'd said. But I was pretty sure he meant he only wanted to be with me if I had sex with him.

"Leona, you need to make up your mind. It's not like you're drop dead gorgeous."

My blood boiled with anger while my skin crawled with disgust. "You and your friends have until *tomorrow at noon* to get the hell out of my house. If you're not out by then, I'll call the cops and file attempted rape charges against you." I grabbed my phone and had my hand on the doorknob.

"You're kidding me, right?"

I stopped and looked back. "Stay until tomorrow and test me."

I slammed the door behind me and hurried down the stairs. On the verge of tears, I didn't want anyone to see. Once I got to the bottom of the stairs, I saw Logan and Emily sitting on the couch, eating. Logan went on full-alert mode.

I came to a stop and shouted, "Shut up, Logan and leave me alone." Logan looked stunned. Emily, with a soft touch, put her hand on his arm and gave him a look. I stomped off to my room.

How could I have been so stupid? I don't know what I'd expected being in a room with him... but I didn't expect that. Oh gosh! I'd just told him to go home. Now I had to find myself a way home. A plane ticket would cost too much. I didn't remember how much I had on my debit card. Bus may be my best bet.

How could I have not seen this coming? Especially after what happened Friday at school. I had just gotten out of art class and I saw Rodney talking to a group of guys in the hallway. I overheard Rodney say, "This week for sure."

"What's going on this week?" I asked.

Rodney looked at me and said, "A hell of a good time."

The guys walked away, smirking.

How could I be such an airhead?

I heard Rodney's crew walking into the house. I could only imagine what he would tell them. I could slap myself.

I laid in my bed, thinking back. There had been plenty of signs and I'd ignored them all. Not to mention Grandma Sue in Hawaii. Eve and the others who never liked him tried to tell me, too.

Oh God, I hope he doesn't stay the night. I don't even want to see him in the morning. I just might hit him with the frying pan.

A knock on the door distracted me. "Come in."

Emily poked her head in. "Leona, sweetheart, your friends are packing the car. Are you guys leaving tonight?"

"*They* are leaving tonight," I corrected her.

She came in and sat on the corner of the bed. "Is this something we need to talk about?"

"Not really. Rodney and I broke up and I told him to leave."

"Did he hurt you?"

"No." She looked at me. "Not physically." She nodded. "Look, I'm going to need you guys to take me to the bus station. I think there is one in Hyannis."

"Are you sure you don't want us to take you home?"

"Emily, I appreciate the gesture, but no. I don't want to be in a car with Logan for four hours. He'll only sit and remind me over and over again that he was right."

She smiled sympathetically. "Okay, well just stay until Saturday. Enjoy the rest of the time with us and we'll send you out first thing Sunday. Does that sound okay with you?"

"Sure."

She asked, "Are you hungry?"

"No, thank you. Emily... I appreciate everything."

After she left, I text Leland. "Hey, are you home yet?"

"Yeah, why?"

I contemplated telling him the truth. "Rodney and I broke up. I'm coming home on the bus Sunday."

"He left you there." I could feel his anger through the text.

"No, I told him to leave. Can you pick me up?"

"What happened?" he asked.

"Can you pick me up or not?"

"Yes, I'll be there to pick you up."

Why didn't I just listen? I'm so stupid.

For several hours, I just remembered things. Things that happened should have clued me in. Warnings people gave me. I'd definitely learned that, if one person doesn't like someone, it's probably a personality clash. But if everyone in your family doesn't like him, then you should listen. Not to mention Grandma Sue. There was no bigger warning than that and I still hadn't listened.

Nevertheless, I was lucky. He could have done what he'd wanted to, anyway. He was easily twice my size. I hate to think what I would have done if Logan wasn't home.

I fell asleep feeling like the biggest idiot in the world.

19

I was embarrassed, angry, hurt, and I don't know what else... anything but happy. I was especially nervous because this would be my first day back to school. I'd never cried so much in my life. Just when I thought life was going well, it had all been torn apart.

The past few days, the words of Grandma Sue keep replaying through my mind. Her warning should have been the one that I paid attention to, but I was so... stubborn.

Talk about the mountain only God can move. I'd say He'd gotten my attention. I was beginning to think that it wasn't determination that got me to Hawaii.

Last night, when the bus pulled up to the station, I saw Maka's car with the both Leland and Maka sitting on the hood. After retrieving my bag, I walked over to them. When I get close, neither had moved. "I have everything I need. Can we go home?"

"Lee," my brother asked. "What happened?"

I sighed in frustration. "Does it matter? The end result is that we broke up."

"It does matter. Word is going around and knowing you, I know it's not the truth. You need to tell me what happened."

"What is everyone saying?" *Time to freak out.*

"Tell me the truth, Leona."

Amazingly, his tone wasn't at all aggressive, more like tender and caring. After a moment, Leland looked at Maka and, without saying a word to each other, Maka got up and walked away. I put my bag in front of the car and sat on the hood.

"What happened?"

I told him everything that happened that day. I started with me waiting for Logan to leave. Just when I thought there were no tears left in me, the waterworks started all over. Everything came out. I noticed Leland stiffen up when I after I told him how I'd poked Rodney in his eye. I finally finished with the whole ugly story. I could tell Leland was furious.

"Leland, just let it go. Please," I begged. "I don't want to deal with this anymore. I don't even want to think about it. I doubt he'll bother me. In the end, he didn't do anything."

"That's not the point." Every muscle in his neck had tightened. His face had changed into an angry mask.

"It's not the first time that I've looked bad." I tried to joke. Leland gave me a look that said he wasn't amused. "Leland, you're going to go to the Marines in three months. You don't want to ruin your chances of joining, do you? If what he's doing is gossiping, then he really hasn't done anything wrong." *Wow, all of a sudden, I'd started sounding like Eve.* "If he starts to bully me in any way, then you'll be the first person I tell. But right now, there isn't much reason to do anything. Please Lee, I'm begging you, let it go."

"Fine," he said, reluctantly. "If his breath even touches you, you'd better tell me."

I nodded and crossed my heart with my index finger.

"There is something else I want to warn you about." I waited for him to continue. "I found out that Rodney has already started dating some chick named Genevieve. Eve says you two aren't the best of friends."

My heart dropped. I really didn't mean anything to him if he'd already hooked up with her.

He pulled out his phone and texted someone. "I just thought you should know."

Maka came back and we headed home, uncomfortable silence filling the car.

～

Being back at school wasn't too bad. A few glances, but that was about it. No one seemed to care to gossip to my face. The bell rang and I went to my locker. Leland walked me to my first class and I could see him, watching me from afar. I ignored him.

"Hey, how's your day going?" I turned and Eve stood next to me. "I'll walk with you to class." She smiled.

Then, Genevieve was there, way too close for comfort. "I just want to warn you to stay away from Rodney. He's mine now," she said.

"So, tell me Gen..." I leaned against my locker. With as much sarcasm as I could muster, I asked, "How long is the standard wait time for girl like you? Twenty-four hours?"

She gasped.

"I'm sure you had to make an exception for Rodney."

She stepped closer to me.

I broke away from the locker and braced myself, but Eve stepped in, keeping Genevieve at a distance. "Okay, relax people." Eve urged.

Gen huffed and left.

Eve gave me a disapproving look my mother would be proud of.

"The old me is back, Eve. I refuse to be bullied."

After English, I walked to art. I have Brazil now, so I immediately started on my project.

"Hey, you." I looked and it was Nick. He was working next to me.

"Hey... can I ask you something?"

"Shoot."

"There's some gossip going around. About me over spring break. Have you heard anything?" I waited.

"I've heard a few things," he said, sitting down at the stool next to me.

"What are they saying? No one will tell me."

He inhaled slowly. "He told everyone that you stripped for him. That when he started doing what you *said* you wanted, you panicked and kicked them out that night."

I was appalled. "Do you believe it?"

Without hesitation, he answered. "No. You're not the type."

Relief. "Thanks."

After art class, Eve met me and walked with me. A few feet away from my locker, someone knocked my books to the floor. Before I had a chance to react, someone bumped me hard enough that I fell against the lockers. I looked up and saw Rodney and Genevieve. I bent down to pick up the books but just then, Rodney fell to the floor, a body on top of him. It took me a split-second, to realize my brother was that body. I inhaled sharply.

"Leland stop it!" But both of them were throwing punches. I doubted Lee could hear me over everyone cheering for a fight. Next, Genevieve jumped on Leland's back, hitting him. Then, I had a handful of Genevieve's hair, yanking her off my brother.

LEE and I sat in Mr. Cavalier's office, waiting for our parents to come and pick us up. I texted Rodney, warning him that if he pressed charges against Leland, he would be facing charges himself. My mother was the first to walk into the office, followed by my dad, and to my surprise, Leland's recruiter and Ms. Lumina.

"So, they will both be suspended for the rest of this week. They

Finding It

can return Monday," Ms. Lumina said. "I'll have to walk each of them to their lockers."

"If you allow me, I can walk Leland to his locker," Staff Sergeant Black volunteered.

"That will be fine, but wait until the other two students have left the school," Ms. Lumina said.

When she left, we sat quietly until Staff Sergeant Black broke the silence. "I would like to have Leland all this week during school hours if you two would allow it."

"What would he be doing all day?" Dad asked.

"I'd like to put him into a few volunteer programs. Keep him busy instead of sitting at home having himself another vacation."

"That sounds good to me." My father's tone was low, but stressed.

Ms. Lumina returned and I walked with her while my parents waited in the office. "You and I will begin counseling sessions again." Ms. Lumina sighed. "I have to say I am disappointed. You seemed to have been doing really well."

I had nothing to say.

∼

WE GOT HOME AND, as Leland and I headed to our rooms, Dad spoke in a stern voice. "Both of you. On the couch."

We turned and sat.

When my mother came through the door, she was the one who broke the silence. "This has to be a record." She paced back and forth. What would possess you to break the kid's nose, Leland? If he presses charges, your future is ruined. You know that, right?"

"Mom, I had a good reason," Leland answered.

"Really?" She cut him off. "What would justify breaking his nose?"

The next words I heard were heartbreaking.

"Leland, what are you doing?" I tried to stop him. I didn't want to relive the horror, or have my parents hear the ugly details.

"Shut up, Leona." He continued to tell Mom about what had happened over spring break. I wanted to disappear. As Leland talked, I glanced up. Dad's face was red. My mom stood still, her mouth hung open. My face fell into my hands. Leland told them *everything*.

"Leona, is this true?" Mom asked. Her voice had softened.

My hesitation in answering told her it was true.

"Sweetheart, why didn't you tell me? I would have understood."

"Really Mom, you think you would have?" I snapped. "This coming from the person who said she was waiting for me to fail."

"I have never said such a thing."

"You didn't say that to Dad in the kitchen after I asked about the Hawaii trip?" My voice had gotten loud.

Her arms fell to her sides, recalling the conversation. My father shifted in his chair.

"That's exactly what I wanted to tell my mother. The very thing that would prove her right." I walked away and locked myself in my room.

An hour later, I heard my father calling me. When I walked into the living room, my heart dropped. Two police officers stood with my parents. One male officer and a female. The male officer spoke first. "My name is Lieutenant Timothy Burg. This is my partner, Sergeant Lukash. We understand something happened last week that you want to report."

I looked back and forth between my parents and the officers. "I'm sorry, but I'm afraid my parents have wasted your time."

"Ms. Sentmore, if someone tried to harm you, you should report it," Lieutenant Burg responded.

"Nothing happened. It's a misunderstanding. Have a good night." I turned to go but didn't get far because I felt a hand gently take my arm.

"Leona." My dad. "You did nothing wrong. You didn't fail at

Finding It

anything. Don't let this kid get away with what he tried to do to you."

I was on the verge of tears again. "He didn't, Dad. Leland broke his nose. Remember?" I shook loose of my father's grip, turned and went back to my room. Within seconds, there was a knock on my door. I opened the door and it was Sergeant Lukash.

"It probably wouldn't be a good idea to slam the door in your face, would it?"

"Probably not. May I come in?" Sergeant Lukash asked.

"Sure."

"My son goes to your school, his name is Dathan. I remember some time ago he said that a girl named Leona stood up for him at lunch. It was just before Thanksgiving. So, you can imagine my surprise when I got this note from him a few nights ago." She placed a Post-it note in front of me. It read: "Listen out for the names Leona Sentmore and Baron Rodney." The letter "V" was written next to my name and a "P" next to Rodney's.

"What's the V and the P stand for?" I asked.

"He is indicating to me who the victim is and who the predator is." She took the note and put it into her pocket. "I can't tell you what to do. But from what your parents and brother told us, you should do something about it. Chances are you aren't his only victim."

The word "victim" sent chills down my spine. "There is nothing to report." I repeated.

"Okay," she said reluctantly. "But if you happen to change your mind, here is my card." She handed me a business card. "Regardless Leona, you should probably find someone to talk to." I nodded and she left.

I cleaned my desk drawers, out with the old. I found the keychain Rodney gave me for my trip to Hawaii, along with ticket stubs from a few of our dates. I wished I had a drink. Then I remembered. I did have a bottle hidden in my closet. Rodney gave me one. I hurried over to my closet and took a drink. Then, another knock on my door. I stashed the bottle and swung opened the door.

"What?"

"It's Eve."

"Sorry, come on in."

"How are you doing?" Eve asked sympathetically.

"I'm doing." I sat back down at my desk as she perched on my bed.

"Well, would you mind if I said something about everything that's happened? I promise it will be the only thing I say, unless you ask me."

I nodded.

"You have a choice right about now."

"What choice would that be?"

"The choice to be *bitter*, or to be *better*." She moved closer. "In the book of Genesis, there was a boy named Joseph. He was hated, betrayed, beaten, sold into slavery, and thrown into jail. But if there is one thing that we can learn from his story, it's what happened when he came face to face with the men who hated him and sold him into slavery. He chose to be bitter for a short while. But it did nothing but allow the weight of what happened to get heavier. It wasn't until he chose to be *better* that God could show, not only him, but his family the light and favor over them."

"You think God can make something of this whole mess?" I asked.

"If you let Him, yes." She half-smiled at me. "I'll see you sometime later this week." And she was gone.

"Okay, God," I said to myself. "If you are real and you want me to go to church or whatever... then I'm going to need you to somehow speak to me and tell me where you want me to go." I can't believe I just did that. I took another drink from the bottle and went back to cleaning my desk.

I was close to the emptying out the drawers when my heart skipped a beat. I pulled out a pamphlet from the Agape Pentecostal

Finding It

Church of God. It was the first thing Eve gave me the night I met her at the pizza diner. This *could* just be a coincidence. I've had the thing for months. I started sorting through the pile of things. I came to an envelope with nothing on it. I opened it up and began to read.

My Child,

I know things are tough right now and you are having a hard time. But you are one of My many creations and there are a few things you should know about yourself.

First, you are a fighter. I have prepared you for every kind of fight there is. Mentally, emotionally, physically, and spiritually. You are well equipped to handle all battles that come your way. If something comes at you and you are not sure what to do, pick up the Bible and start reading. I will lead you to the right answer.

Ignore all negativity. Know that you are worth more than rubies and that all things are possible through Me. Allow Me to guide you and take refuge in the peace that I set into your life. Do just that and you will be a success.

Aside from what many may say, you are a light and an instrument and I will prove them wrong. Push and exceed the limits you've set for yourself. It's okay to take a few breaks but jump right back onto the task. Don't get distracted and don't procrastinate. Love your goal but love the process even more. Remember that anything that is hard to obtain is much more appreciated. There is a blessing on the other side and you will have to fight to get there. Don't let your guard down and always be ready for the unexpected.

Long-term consistency is better the short-term intensity. Stand firm, my child, when all is over you will be more than just content.
Love Always,
Your Heavenly Father

. . .

I didn't know why but I was crying again. "Okay," I said to myself. "I'll go to the Agape Church. But I won't go if Eve is going to be there. She'll smother me." I picked up my phone and texted Maka. "Don't tell Eve that I am texting you."

"Okay, what's up?"

"Are you going to church this week?"

"Yeah, next service is Wednesday night."

"Will Eve be going with you?"

"Yes."

"No offense to your sister, but I doubt she'll be able to keep my going to church quiet."

"She'll be away at a retreat this weekend but we have another service both nights from seven to nine-thirty."

"Would you mind picking me up for those? I would like to go."

"Sure, I'll pick you up by six-forty-five."

"Okay, don't tell anyone please."

"See you then."

I put the letter back in its envelope and back in my desk. A shower and then to bed. I wasn't really sure about what I'd decided to do. But I think it was what I'd prayed for.

20

I'd been nervous all day. I was sitting in front of my computer finishing up some homework Eve brought over for me yesterday.

Mom spoke with me a few days ago. She was trying to apologize. Mom even said that Dad spoke to the recruiter and told him that there were extenuating circumstances and about how Leland was defending me. Leland made me promise not to date anyone until after he leaves for the Marines. I agreed.

My mother popped her head in my open door. "Maka is here to pick you up. Are you sure you don't want to eat something before your movie?"

"No, Mom. I'm sure." I wasn't ready to tell anyone I was going to church. *Just yet.*

Downstairs, I saw Maka. "Hey."

"If you like, we could stop after to eat something. Is that okay, Mrs. Sentmore?"

"That is fine by me," she answered.

We got to the church and I declined sitting with Maka and his friends. I sat by myself, second row from the back.

The service started much like the one from Hawaii had. Singing, then more singing for the offering, then the guy preaching.

"Today, I am going to bring the Word a little more differently. I have been getting many calls about people finding themselves in valleys. Some valleys are harder to walk through than others, but these valleys are always a low point in our lives. It doesn't matter whether you are a believer of Christ or not, you will always walk a valley.

A valley that I've walked through was back in 2002, where, in eight months, terrible things happened. My father passed away. My mom's parents passed away, a month apart from each other. I was expecting a child and my wife got into a car accident and the stress from the accident caused her to miscarry. To top it all off, from the stress of everything, I ended up in the hospital with a mild heart attack.

The thing about going from valley to valley is that you will also go from mountain top to mountain top. But something you should remember is that you can never appreciate the height of your victory if you have never fully comprehended the depths of your struggle.

He continued, talking about verses in the Bible and the significance of them. He kept my undivided attention. I almost felt like I was the only one in the room. My body had found more water to make tears.

At the end, he asked everyone to stand. I stood. I felt compelled to do more. I want to scream and tell God that I was paying attention. I wanted to tell Him that I was listening. I wanted Him to tell me what to do. Where does He want me to go from here?

So, whether your valley is a bad day, a family issue, or a personal one, remember that there is a mountain top. But the decision is up to you, when you get to the mountain top, you'll look back. Are you just going to be relieved that it's all over? Or are you going to realize how far you have come and that God had never left. The altar is open for those who would like prayer.

TEARS STREAMING DOWN MY FACE, I fought with myself about going up for prayer. If I went up, people were going to see me. But I haven't stopped crying, that meant I needed prayer, right? But what would the point be in going for prayer? I mean, I would have to stop drinking, right? My attitude was definitely not where it should be.

God, you got my attention, but at this point I can't do anything for You. I'll come again to church, but for prayer, to accept that I have to fix a few things first.

AFTER THE SERVICE, Maka and I walked down the street to the pizza parlor. The inside was packed, but this time, there were some tables and chairs set up along the sidewalk. Maka pointed to a table outside. We discovered there was only one chair at the table. He walked away to order our food and find another chair.

I sat down. I couldn't help but feel like I've still done something or was doing something wrong. I hung my head. Hearing the scrape of a chair being dragged, I thought, *That was fast.* Assuming it was Maka, I looked up to see it was Damiano. He sat, leaning back in the chair, making himself at home.

"What do you want?" I asked, completely annoyed.

"I'm just upset I missed the fight. Sounded good." He smiled his sleazy smile.

"You know, vermin like you that popup unwelcome, normally don't last long in the wild," I said. "Maybe you should think twice about being one."

"From what I hear, you're the one that likes to be wild."

I did my best to inherit my father's poker face, but I doubted it worked.

He sat up with his elbows on the table and leaned in. "What do you say if I find us a place so you can show me what you got. You know... just for observation purposes." He winked.

"What are you doing here, Dom?" Maka asked.

"Oh, Maka, you're with her. Tell me, is the show worth the time?"

Maka shoved Domiano. The chair tilted back and Dom landed on the ground. Maka stood over him. I leaped forward and grabbed hold of Maka's arm.

"Maka, no." I looked at him earnestly. "Please Maka, don't."

He breathed hard a few times and nodded. "Get out of here, Dom. Now."

Domiano got up, dusted himself off, and left. When he was a good bit away, I let go of Maka's arm. I sat down and covered my face. Maka picked up the chair and sat down.

"Sorry," he said. "You're taking a lot of nonsense from people and you don't deserve it."

"I have to worry about Leland facing charges. I don't want to have to worry about you, too." I said, staring at the sidewalk.

"Leland won't be facing any charges."

"How do you know?"

"I don't know how she knows, but Athena Mainard spoke to Eve and me in school. She said that Rodney's parents grounded him and took his phone. They saw a text you sent him about facing charges himself. She said she didn't know any details, but because of that text they decided not to press charges."

"They probably don't want to find out what a monster their son is."

"Probably."

The pizza showed up, signaling a change in conversation.

"Why didn't you go to that retreat thing that Eve went to?"

"I didn't want to go this year. I haven't gone for three years now."

"Oh." I took a bite of pizza.

"Will you be going to service tomorrow?" Maka asked.

I thought it through while I still had food in my mouth. "I think I might," I finally answered. "I don't know, I just can't seem to make sense of my thoughts or my feelings." I sighed. "I should have listened to Grandma Sue," I said, under my breath.

"Grandma Sue? What does she have to do with any of this?" Maka asked, intrigued.

"She said to break up with Rodney. I probably should have listened but didn't."

Maka nodded his head as he finished chewing. "Yeah, that's happened to me once or twice. But you can't beat yourself up about it. Nothing that has happened is your fault." He shifted in his seat. "Leona, if I know Grandma Sue, chances are she gave you that message telling you that God or Jesus lead her to say it."

I nodded.

Maka's voice was gentle and sincere. "Then you have had an experience where God had spoken into your life even before accepting Him. Do you honestly think it was you who convinced your parents to let you go on that trip? Leona, you're worth dying for."

I looked down at my pizza, trying to contain my emotions.

"Would you like me to pray for you?"

"You know, I wanted to go up for prayer tonight, but I couldn't. I'm just tired of doing what's wrong. I mean, for the first time, I am giving God some consideration, but how can He love me when I just now am giving Him a thought?" I started crying again, harder.

"You know when a mother gives birth? Her love isn't dependent on the child loving her back. Her love is unconditional, even though the baby has no recollection of who she is. She loves it. In time, the baby will grow and learn the he loves her too, but until then, her love is this baby's foundation. God is Mom, you are the baby." After a brief moment he asked, "Leona, would you like to accept Jesus as your Lord and Savior?"

I nodded.

"Okay, repeat after me."

We closed our eyes and bowed our heads. "God, thank You for calling me." I repeated the words. "I am sorry that I took so long to answer." I repeated. "But I find myself here, knowing that You are real." I echoed Maka's words and the tears started to flow even faster. "Knowing that Jesus was sacrificed for my sins." I repeated. "Thank you for Jesus and I accept Him as my Savior." I said with tears streaming down my face. "In Jesus' name... amen."

"In Jesus' name, amen."

"God, I thank You for this beautiful woman. I pray that You will strengthen her and guide her. Fill her with Your love and wipe away her tears. Help her find peace in all this chaos. She is Yours and You are hers. Have Your way in her life. In Jesus' name, amen."

We kept talking for a while, then he took me home. When I got into bed, I started thinking about one of the things the pastor had spoken about. He said, "The best way to make it through those valleys was to pray your way through it." I got back up and kneeled next to my bed.

"GOD, *I don't really know how this works, but I know You can help me. I don't really know what to ask for, either. I just know that life isn't as good as it probably could be. I feel better but I still feel like something is missing. Can You, like, somehow let me know that what I did tonight was right? I'm kind of tired of doing the wrong thing. But now that I have You, or now that You're my Savior, if I am doing what's right, provide me, God, with a Bible, if you will. I would appreciate it. Ummm... in Jesus' name, amen."*

I DON'T KNOW if I ended that right, but Maka ended each prayer that way. I hope it was right. I got back into bed and fell asleep with the most tranquility I'd had in weeks.

21

I'd been back at school for a week. It hadn't been too bad. I got a few glares from certain people, but they didn't approach me. Athena told me that as long as Leland was around, no one from that group would bother me.

A few people mentioned that I seemed happier and that I carried a glow with me. I asked Maka what that meant. He said that when the presence of God comes upon people, they glow. Wow, and I could read about something like that happening to Moses in the book of Exodus. But I was still waiting on the Bible I'd asked for.

I haven't been back to church. I wanted to go. I just wasn't sure about going with Eve. It sounded bad, but I was so new to this and I knew she'd smother me with Bible verses and other things I should and shouldn't do. I didn't know if I was ready for that yet.

Unfortunately, Logan was right. I hadn't gone a day without drinking at least one shot of alcohol. I realized it when I finished my stash in the closet. I paid someone to buy me a bottle. I haven't brought a drink to school but at home I mixed it with juice and drank it. Before long, I had a bottle of mixed juice and alcohol with me, at school.

I felt kind of stressed out. The art show was about to start. They had my project on a small stage. On the stage was something that looked like a voter's booth without a curtain. At the stairs of the entrance to the stage was a sign that said, "Perfect Grade Winner."

People poured into the gym and my nerves were on edge. I finished the bottle and threw it into a trash can nearby. The Aquinos and my family were the first to walk over. My parents, the Aquinos and Leland went to examine my project. I put mint gum in my mouth. They each complimented me, then walked around looking at the other projects.

Maka stayed behind. "I was wondering something. You said you go a different service on Sunday than Eve does."

"Right."

"Do you mind if I go with you this Sunday?"

"Not at all." Maka looked a little nervous. "Listen, I have to apologize to you."

I looked at him, puzzled.

"I kind of let it slip to my mother that I took you to church last week. I told her that you didn't want anyone to know just yet and she promised she wouldn't say anything."

"People are going to find out. It's okay. Just let me tell Eve."

"That's fair." Ever since Maka came to pick me up at the bus station, I've been seeing a different side to him. I liked it.

Just then, Ethan and May walked up together to see my project. Maka watched along with me. May said something to Ethan and he laughed. Coming down the stairs, she looked at me and rolled her eyes in disgust. Ethan was still laughing.

"Do you want me to stay with you?" Maka asked.

"No, I'll be fine."

"Let me know if you need anything." He walked away.

When the art show was over, we all met up at my house. We played board games. I can't play Scrabble against my mother or Mrs. Aquino. I never win. It was the same thing on New Year's Eve.

When the night came to an end, I said *goodbye* and went to my room. Shortly after, there was a soft knock on my door.

"Come in."

It was Mrs. Aquino. "I hope you don't mind my stopping by real quick. But I have something for you." She opened her very large purse and pulled out a book. "I believe you need one of these." She placed it on my desk. "Good night, Leona."

"G'night." She left. I finished putting on my pajamas and walked over to my desk. When I looked to see what book she'd left me. I started to cry. The title read: "NIV Teen Study Bible."

I kneeled down and prayed.

"Thank you, God for my Bible. I know I have a lot of work to do, but I know now that You also listen to me. I'm sorry for doubting and I'm pretty sure the drinking is bad, too. But like You said, I'm stubborn and my change won't be overnight. Thank You for coming into my life. Thank You for filling me with Your glow. I can't wait to see what You do next. In Jesus' name, amen."

I brushed my teeth and got into bed. I laid there and I couldn't help but realize how much easier the past few days had been. How such a small request for a Bible was heard and answered. But now that I'd accepted Jesus as my Lord and Savior... what next?

ABOUT THE AUTHOR

Wanda Torres was born to Rafael Fuentes and Wanda Ortiz in the Bronx, New York. She was the third of three girls. In June 29, 2013, she married Rolando Torres Jr. They have three amazing children.

Wanda and her family live in Tampa, Florida. She serves at her church as the director of the ushers, on the prayer team, and as an ASL interpreter.

When she's not writing, at church, or chasing after one of her daughters, she loves to crochet and enjoys time with her family doing outdoor activities. She also has a passion for various arts and crafts.

The best day of her life was on June 30, 2006, when she accepted Jesus as her Lord and Savior. In June 18, 2018, she graduated from Mizpa Christian University.

Her passion is to reach young girls and help them through the many trials they face these days.

To invite Wanda to speak to your youth group, women's retreat, school, or church, reach out to her at:

Email: wandat.2019@outlook.com

Facebook, Twitter, and Instagram: wandafoundit

"I'm ever grateful to God for what He has done in me and through me. I can't wait to see and hear what He does next in my life!" Wanda Torres

www.ingramcontent.com/pod-product-compliance
Lightning Source LLC
Chambersburg PA
CBHW052037070526
44584CB00016B/2081